Skills for Study

LEVEL 2

Craig Fletcher

Series editor: Ian Smallwood

CAMBRIDGE UNIVERSITY PRESS
Cambridge, New York, Melbourne, Madrid, Cape Town,
Singapore, São Paulo, Delhi, Mexico City

Cambridge University Press
The Edinburgh Building, Cambridge CB2 8RU, UK

www.cambridge.org
Information on this title: www.cambridge.org/9781107611290

First published 2012

Printed and bound in the United Kingdom by the MPG Books Group

A catalogue record for this publication is available from the British Library

ISBN 978-1-107-61129-0 Paperback

Acknowledgements
The authors and publishers acknowledge the following
sources of copyright material and are grateful for the
permissions granted. While every effort has been made, it
has not always been possible to identify the sources of all
the material used, or to trace all copyright holders. If any
omissions are brought to our notice, we will be happy to
include the appropriate acknowledgements on reprinting.

Author acknowledgements
The authoring team would like to thank Clare Sheridan,
Ian Morrison, Nick Robinson, Nik White, Sarah Curtis,
Chris Capper and Ian Collier for their constant help and
support throughout the whole project. We also offer
our grateful acknowledgement to Carolyn Gibbs, Claire
Ashmore, Fred Gooch, and Neil McSweeney for their
advice and contributions to the manuscripts. We would
like to thank staff and teachers at Kaplan International
Colleges who have been involved with the development
of the course.

Publisher acknowledgements
The authors and publishers would like to thank the
following people who reviewed and commented on the
material at various stages: Michael McCarthy, Jenifer
Spencer, Dr Mike Courtney and Debbie Goldblatt.

Design and illustrations by Hart McLeod, Cambridge

Photo acknowledgements
p.4© Neustockimages/istockphotos.com, ©Christine
Osborne Pictures/Alamy, ©Huw Jones/Alamy, ©Steven
May/Alamy; p.7 ©Neustockimages/istockphotos.com;
p.63 ©Simon Belcher/Alamy, ©Felix Brandl/istockphoto.
com, ©filonmar/istockphoto.com; p.66 ©Christine Osborne
Pictures/Alamy; p.137 ©Huw Jones / Alamy; p.191 ©Steven
May/Alamy; p.200 A ©The Art Gallery Collection/Alamy
B ©Lebrecht Music and Arts Photo Library/Alamy, C
©Ancient Art & Architecture Collection Ltd/Alamy; p.203
l Andreas Praefcke, 2007 http://commons.wikimedia.org/
wiki/File:Claux_de_Werve_St_Barbara.jpg, r ©Erin Babnik/
Alamy; p.208 ©Paul S. Bartholomew/Alamy

Skills for study Contents

Map of the book

	Part A Understanding spoken information	Part B Understanding written information
1 Gender issues	Understanding descriptions of data in spoken language Understanding references to graphic data Understanding and evaluating a speaker's interpretation of data	Recognizing patterns and trends in data Understanding graphic presentations of data Evaluating, comparing and critically analysing graphic data Incorporating graphic information and data into writing
> UNIT TASK Gender issues		
2 Water	Following seminar discussions Comparing and synthesizing ideas and arguments	Finding texts which are at a suitable academic level for your needs Skim reading a report to decide if it suits your purpose Identifying different types of written report Reading feasibility/recommendation reports
> UNIT TASK Water		
3 Progress	Following descriptions of processes and sequences Following an account of the development of ideas over time Following a description of a manufacturing process Following a description of a lab procedure	Following written processes Interpreting process diagrams and flow charts Evaluating processes Critically analysing reported statistics
> UNIT TASK Progress		
4 Art, creativity and design	Coping with distractions Detecting a speaker's level of certainty Listening critically	Identifying appropriate reading techniques Reading intensively for understanding Reading critically
> UNIT TASK Art, creativity and design		
Good study practice checklists **Appendices**		

Part C Investigating	Part D Reporting in speech	Part E Reporting in writing
Preparing a list of references Using secondary citations Keeping records of research	Discussing the meaning and implications of numerical data Using statistical data in support of claims Referring to graphics in support of claims	Identifying different types of report Understanding the core features of a typical written report Writing a literature review Building paragraphs in academic writing Creating a poster to report results
Understanding the research process Understanding primary and secondary research Analysing the process of choosing a research question Writing research proposals	Participating in seminar discussions Exchanging and challenging ideas appropriately in academic discussion Expressing and defending opinions Changing the direction of a discussion Concluding a discussion	Understanding the main features of a primary research report Understanding the main features of a successful feasibility/recommendation report Making choices about the best way to structure your reports
Drawing conclusions from data Dealing with sources of uncertainty Avoiding absolute terms Protecting your position through citation Using cautious language for your own claims	Explaining the possible implications of events Giving an oral progress report	Explaining, comparing and interpreting sources Synthesizing sources and viewpoints Writing a progress report
Understanding reliability and validity Analysing the suitability of samples	Describing research findings Describing and explaining data Discussing research findings	Using supporting information in writing Writing an abstract Avoiding plagiarism

Introduction
Developing your academic skills

Before you start to use this book, complete the questionnaire.
Decide how strongly you agree or disagree with each statement by ticking (✓) the column (1–5) which best describes your opinion according to the following scale:

1 = strongly disagree	3 = neither agree nor disagree
2 = disagree	4 = agree
	5 = strongly agree

Using and interpreting data

		1	2	3	4	5
1	I can understand graphics and tables more easily than text.					
2	I can critically evaluate data in graphics and tables.					
3	I can understand the strong and weak points of different styles of graphics and tables.					
4	I can create effective graphics and tables to present information.					

Discussion skills

5	I have attended seminar discussions.					
6	I can actively participate in seminar and small group discussions.					
7	I can use different strategies to participate in group discussions.					
8	I can understand a group discussion, even when several people are talking.					

Writing skills

9	I understand the difference between a report and an essay.					
10	I have written a report on my subject.					
11	I know what types of reports are used in my subject.					
12	I can synthesize information from different sources in my writing.					
13	I know how to write a literature review.					

Research

14	I can find sources of data which are suitable for my needs.					
15	I can write citations and references in an accepted format.					
16	I know the difference between primary and secondary research.					
17	I understand how to plan a research project.					

Unit 1 Gender issues

Unit overview

Part	This part will help you to ...	By improving your ability to ...
A	**Understand data presented in lectures**	• understand descriptions of data in spoken language • understand references to graphic data • understand and evaluate a speaker's interpretation of data.
B	**Understand and evaluate data and graphics**	• recognize patterns and trends in data • understand graphic presentations of data • evaluate, compare and critically analyze graphic data • incorporate graphic information and data into writing.
C	**Keep accurate records of your research**	• prepare a list of references • use secondary citations • keep records of research.
D	**Contribute to discussions**	• discuss the meaning and implications of numerical data • use statistical data in support of claims • refer to graphics in support of claims.
E	**Write standard academic reports**	• identify different types of report • understand the core features of a typical written report • write a literature review • build paragraphs in academic writing • create a poster to report results.

The Unit 1 task is about the gender gap. At the end of each part, you will be asked to complete a stage of the task as follows:

Part A: Listen to an introduction on the topic.

Part B: Read two texts about it.

Part C: Do some further research for relevant material.

Part D: Have a group discussion on the topic.

Part E: Write an essay with one of these titles:

Assignment 1
Thinking only about economic opportunities, give an overview of the progress made towards gender equality over the last decade. You may concentrate on a single country of your choice, or you may consider this from a global perspective.

Assignment 2
Compare the gender gap in higher education in two countries of your choice.

Assignment 3
Compare male and female rates of participation in STEM (science, technology, engineering and mathematics) subjects. Identify possible reasons for any differences between participation rates.

a You are going to listen to a lecturer talking about different aspects of the gender gap around the world. Before you listen, work in small groups to consider these questions.

　　1 What kinds of gender gap are you aware of in your own society?

　　2 Do you think educational and occupational gender gaps will ever be completely eliminated?

　　3 What do you think the ratio of female to male politicians is in your own society?

b You are going to listen to this lecture to help you think of things to contribute to a discussion on the topic of the gender gap. The lecture will help you to discover other possible sources of information and focus your own ideas. Listen to the first part of the lecture and take notes on the framework the lecturer used in her research in the table on p.15.

1.7

c Now listen to the second part of the lecture. Make a note of the speaker's claims about the status of women in society and the gender gap overall.

1.8

Notes on the gender gap

Methodology/framework:

Key information	Supporting data or statistics	Names of other sources of information
Claims about the status of women in society: Health and primary education –		
Tertiary education –		
Economic opportunities –		
Political participation –		
Gender parity across different regions and countries –		
Claims about the gender gap overall:		

d Spend some time reflecting on your notes; compare what you have heard in this lecture with other information about the gender gap that you have discovered while working through Part A. Discuss your ideas with your group and then add any new comments, questions or ideas to the notes.

Go to the checklist on p.241 and read the tips relating to Unit 1 Part A.

Understanding written information

By the end of Part B you will be able to:

- recognize patterns and trends in data
- understand graphic presentations of data
- evaluate, compare and critically analyze graphic data
- incorporate graphic information and data into writing.

1 Recognizing patterns and trends in data

1a Work in small groups. You are going to read about the gender gap in higher education. Before you begin, look at the words and phrases below. How might they relate to the gender gap in higher education?

51%	63%	education courses	engineering courses	increasing
	outnumber	senior professors	under-represented	

1b In this section you will look for trends in the data about gender that you heard in Part A. Skim read through the texts below to check if your predictions in 1a were correct.

A The last two to three decades have seen a great improvement in gender equality in higher education, with more women overall studying in all fields. The percentage of all students who are female has risen from around 45% in the mid-1980s to just over 50% at the time of writing, a figure which is predicted to keep increasing over the next 20 years (OECD, 2008). Nevertheless, there is still a gender gap of sorts in the types of subjects which male and female students tend to study. Male students are clearly in the majority on science and engineering courses, with around 60% of all science degrees and approximately 74% of all engineering degrees awarded to male students in a study of 29 nations conducted by the OECD (2008). Female students, on the other hand, greatly outnumber their male peers in subjects which are seen as being more traditionally 'female'; in education courses, for instance, just over 76% of all degrees were awarded to female students according to the same OECD report.

B Overall, the global trend for greater numbers of female students in higher education continues. A recent UNESCO report (2009) estimates that 51% of all students in higher education around the world are female. A number of studies suggest that this trend will continue throughout the next quarter century, with some estimates putting the percentage of female students as high as 63% by 2025 (OECD, 2008).

C The so-called gender gap in education has traditionally been taken to mean relative imbalances in educational opportunities between the two genders, with men enjoying more advantage and opportunity, and a negative situation for female students. While this continues to be the case in certain sectors and in certain areas of the world (for more information see, for instance, the WEF's 2009 Global Gender Gap Report (WEF, 2009)), it appears that the situation is rather different in higher education, where in fact it is increasingly male students who are under-represented. According to figures published recently by the European Commission (2009), men now only account for about 41% of all university graduates across the 27 member nations of the European Union. Despite the advantage that women seem to hold in terms of graduate numbers, significant negative gaps exist for females in academia. For instance, despite the relatively higher number of female graduates, the difference between the numbers of senior professors of different genders is stark: only 18% of full senior professors are female (EC, 2009, p.75).

1c Read the texts again. Make notes on the claims that the authors make, and any supporting evidence that they give for them.

1d Compare the evidence from the three sources in your notes. Work in pairs. Use the evidence from all three texts to discuss these questions about the overall pattern in the data.

    1 Judging from the data given above, how equal are men and women around the world in terms of higher education?

    2 In what ways is the situation likely to change over the next few decades?

    3 What types of negative gender gaps exist (for either sex)?

1e Read texts from two more sources on this topic. As you read, take notes on the authors' claims and supporting information they give.

> **A**
>
> Another area in which gender inequality seems to persist is women's leadership of academic institutions. Until relatively recently, so little attention was paid to this area of the gender equality issue that data was very scarce (Morley & Lugg, 2009, p.39); however, a number of recent studies suggest that men predominate among senior academic staff. According to one study by Singh (2008, cited in Morley & Lugg, 2009, p.39), which considered female leadership of universities in the Commonwealth[1], over 90% of all universities were headed by men, and men lead all universities in slightly over 65% of all Commonwealth countries.
>
> ---
>
> [1]The Commonwealth of Nations (usually known just as the Commonwealth) is an organization of 54 nations which are, mainly, former members of the British Empire. The Commonwealth nations attempt to abide by and promote shared values. They also cooperate in economic, trade, legal and social matters.

> **B**
>
> Though numbers of female students have increased dramatically over the past three decades, there is still significant gender segregation between different levels of academic staff at universities throughout the world. In Europe in 2006, only 44% of newly qualified academic staff recruited (Grade C) were female. At Grade B, only 36% of staff were female, and this dropped to just 18% of senior (Grade A) professors (European Commission, 2009). In terms of university leadership, also, men tend to be significantly over-represented: on average only 13% of universities or higher education institutions in the EU were headed by women in 2007 (European Commission, ibid).

1f Overall, what trends does the data from 1b and 1e suggest about the gender gap in higher education?

1g Compare your ideas with a partner.

1h Work in small groups. Discuss your answers to these questions about the data.

    1 What similarities are there between female academics in the EU and Commonwealth?

    2 Comparing the data from the passages in 1b and 1e above, to what extent do you agree with this statement?

    A gender gap exists in higher education which benefits males significantly more than females.

2 Understanding graphic presentations of data

> Numerical data presented in a table allows for detailed analysis; presenting the same data in a graphic can be a more striking and memorable way of communicating the information to the reader.
>
> The benefits of presenting ideas in graphics are:
>
> **a** data in graphics can easily illustrate main ideas, patterns and trends.
> **b** presenting numerical data in graphics is often more concise than presenting the same information in text.

Identifying main trends

2a What aspects of a job are most important to you? Rank these aspects from 1 (most important) to 7 (least important).

- 6 **a** Promotion opportunities
- 1 **b** Job satisfaction
- 3 **c** Salary and benefits
- 5 **d** Status
- 7 **e** Travel
- 2 **f** Good work/life balance
- 4 **g** Being valued by your employer

2b Read the introduction to a study and look at the graphics (Figures 4 and 5) below. Work in pairs. Answer these questions about main trends in the data.

> Students carried out a survey to find out whether males and females had similar opinions about what aspects of a job were important to them. Approximately 6,000 people (3,000 men and 3,000 women) took part in the survey.

1 Overall, what aspects of a job do female employees tend to prefer, according to the data?

2 To what extent have women's preferences changed between 1995 and 2009?

3 Overall, what aspects of a job do men seem to consider most important?

4 How have men's preferences changed between 1995 and 2009?

5 To what extent are men's and women's work preferences similar?

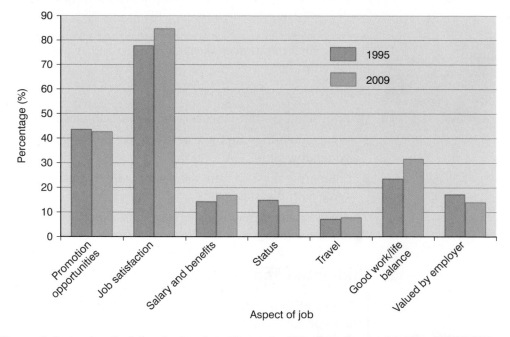

Figure 4: Aspects of a job rated as 'very important' by female employees, 1995/2009

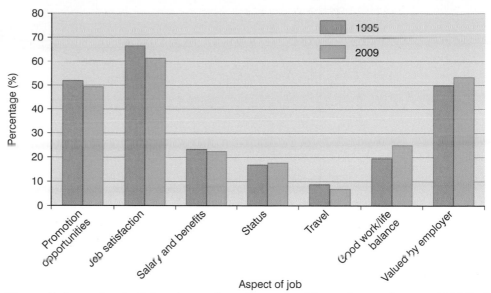

Figure 5: Aspects of a job rated as 'very important' by male employees, 1995/2009

2c To what extent do you agree with the findings above? Find out if male and female members of your class share the same ideas about work preferences.

3   Evaluating, comparing and critically analyzing graphic data

Though graphics are a compelling way of presenting data, it is still important to take a critical view of the data they contain and the way the data is presented. This means being able to question the purpose of the data, whether the data sufficiently supports any claims made by the author, and comparing similar data in other graphics, or from other sources.

Judging how well the data supports the author's claim

3a Work in pairs. Student A reads Text 1 below, and Student B reads Text 2. Identify the author's claim in each text, and then tell your partner what the claim is.

1 A lot of attention has been paid to the gap in earnings between men and women. While it is undeniable that a gap exists, the reasons are less certain. For example, one possible explanation is that women are more likely to choose careers such as education, social care and healthcare, where salaries are lower than in the career paths typically favoured by men, leading to lower overall average salaries for women (see Figure 6).

2 The gender wage gap is evident throughout the entire working life of the individual. Except for a brief period around the ages of 16 to 17, when female teenagers earn slightly more than their male counterparts, males earn consistently more than females, on average. This trend becomes most pronounced in the 40–49 and 50–59 age groups (see Figure 7).

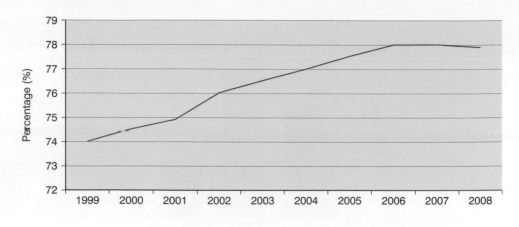

Source: Office for National Statistics (ONS), Annual Survey of Hours and Earnings, 2009

Figure 6: Females earnings as a percentage of male earnings

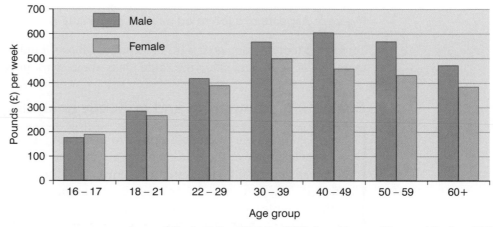

Source: Office for National Statistics (ONS), Annual Survey of Hours and Earnings, 2009

Figure 7: Weekly earnings by age group, 2009

3b Compare each claim with the data presented in the accompanying graphic. How well does the data support the claim? Explain your findings to your partner.

Critically evaluating the design of a graphic

> Sometimes, it is helpful to question whether the design of the graphic is suitable. Good graphics should allow for comparison and analysis of data and present information in a clear and honest way. However, the way in which a graphic is presented can make it difficult to read the numerical values it presents accurately.

3c Work in pairs. At the top of page 21 are two alternative visual representations of men and women's average working hours (from Figure 8, shown at the bottom on page 21). Compare the two charts. The numerical data is exactly the same but it is presented differently. What is the difference?

1 Try to estimate the exact number of hours worked in each of the columns.

2 How easy is it to judge the exact number of hours worked in each column from the two figures?

3 What difference could this make to the way you read the number of hours worked?

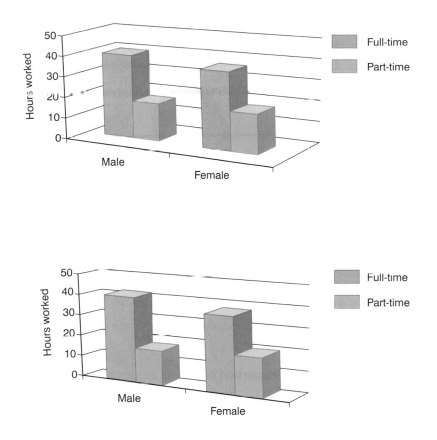

3d Compare your estimates of the numerical data in the two representations of Figure 8 with the two-dimensional chart below. The numerical data is exactly the same but it is presented differently. What is your estimate of the values for each column now?

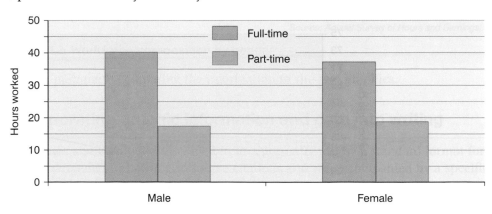

Source: Office for National Statistics (ONS), Annual Survey of Hours and Earnings, 2009

Figure 8: Average weekly paid hours of work, 2009

Investigating

By the end of Part C you will be able to:

- prepare a list of references
- use secondary citations
- keep records of research.

1 Preparing a list of references

1a Work in small groups. How many reasons can you think of for including citations and references? Make a note of your ideas, then read the text that follows to check your answers.

> Accurate referencing is a vital part of successful academic writing. There are several reasons for this, though perhaps the most common is to give proper acknowledgement to an author whose ideas you have used. The author of an original idea is the owner both of the idea, and of the words that were used to express it; an in-text citation and a reference to the original author's work are the way that this acknowledgement is normally given. There are other reasons for using citations and references, too: the person who is reading your work may want to check the original sources of ideas or data which you have used – providing a reference helps them to locate the source easily. Another reason for providing references, one which is particularly important for student writers, is to show your teachers that your work is supported by ideas and information from appropriate academic sources. Finally, citations are useful to help your reader understand which ideas are your own, and which have come from other sources – this is particularly important when your teachers expect you to produce work which is original.

> Any written work you submit must express your own understanding of a topic, written in your own words. However, you will sometimes have to refer to work by other authors for these purposes:
>
> - to support your own opinions
> - to show where key ideas, terms or methods originated
> - to present contrasting opinions for discussion or comparison
> - to demonstrate that you have done relevant research
> - to show you have understood and evaluated different information sources
> - to demonstrate an understanding of the contemporary concerns in that field of study.
>
> The writers whose texts and ideas you have used deserve proper acknowledgement for their contribution to your work. The ideas and work of other researchers must be acknowledged twice in the paper: when you mention their work in the text (an in-text citation or in-text reference) and once (only) in the reference list at the end of your paper. (Similarly, an academic presentation using software like PowerPoint should include citations for supporting data and a final slide of references.)
>
> Citations appear in the main body of the work. Each citation must correspond to a reference in the final list of references and vice versa: the final reference list should only include sources which have been cited in the main body.

1b Look at the example citations in the text below and the excerpt from the list of references which follows it. Work in pairs and answer these questions.

1 Compare the citations in the text below with the accompanying references. What is missing from the final reference list?

2 What is the difference in the information required in a citation and in a reference?

There is still considerable debate about the reasons why different nations have better or worse male-female equality. It has been suggested that equality in terms of health, education and political representation is a consequence of deliberate action by governments which are willing to set policies which protect equality and make it a legal obligation to treat both genders equally (Irwin, 2001, p.15). This view is by no means accepted by all, however. Harrison (2008) claims that the nations which have the greatest male-female equality (i.e. the narrowest gender gap) tend to have a strong cultural inclination towards equality as a principle and are the most likely to enshrine their cultural values in law. It is for this reason, Harrison argues, that the governments of those nations which tend not to have a strong cultural attachment to the idea of gender equality are unlikely to take positive action to enhance equality.

List of references

Gluck, M. (2009). Reframing gender within the context of culture: looking in all the wrong places? *Gender, Society and Development, 24*, 201–225. Retrieved from http://tse.lib.marl.edu.uk/index.php/gsd

Hope, B. & Tilly, J. (2004). *Work and the negative gender gap*. London: Tarsus.

Idle, T. (1998). *Making employment work for all: gender, wealth and life outcomes.* Vancouver: AAP.

Irwin, R. (2001). The role of policy decisions in gender equity in employment. *Journal of Economic and Social Development, 13*(2), 11–29.

Policy Research Institute, Australia. (2009). *National Gender Equity Report 2009.* Retrieved from http://www.pria.org/documents/reports/09_gender.pdf

---

Writing a reference correctly

Different universities, and quite often different departments within a single university, tend to have their own preferred referencing styles. These may be well-known standard styles, such as 'author-date' styles like APA, or 'author-title' styles like MLA, but they may also be styles used only within that institution. It is important to ask your course tutors what referencing style they expect you to use. There are three basic steps to follow in order to write a reference correctly:

| Find out what referencing style you should use | → | Check what type of source you are referencing | → | Find out what information a reference for that source type should contain |

4　A document titled 'Women's Rights', written by Anup Shah. Published online on a Webpage titled 'Global Issues', on 14 March 2010.

http://www.globalissues.org/article/166/womens-rights

5　A chapter titled 'Who works? Comparing Labor Market Practices', written by Wallace Clement. It appeared in a book titled 'Reconfigurations of class and gender', edited by Janeen Baxter and Mark Webster, published in 2001, in Stanford, by Stanford University Press. Clement's article appeared on pages 55–80.

6　A report titled 'Gender equality scheme annual report 2009', written and published by the Scottish Government, in Edinburgh, 2009.

7　A book titled 'Masculinities', written by Raewyn Connell. Published in 2005, by Polity Press, in Cambridge.

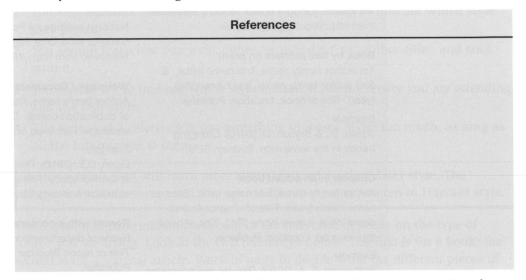

References

1g　Before your next lesson, try to find the following things. Get prints or copies of them and bring them to your next class.

1　Find out if your department or subject tutor has a reference style sheet that they prefer to use.

2　Find out what guides to writing references are available in your university or university library.

A note on DOI (Digital Object Identifiers)

Online publishing is becoming more common all the time, and the rules for how to refer to academic articles and books published online are changing. Traditionally, the reference for a text found online includes the web address (URL) at the end.

Example

Burns, N. (2005). Finding Gender. *Politics and Gender*, 1, 137–141. Retrieved from http://journals.cambridge.org/action/displayIssue?jid = PAG&volumeId = 1& issueId = 01

However, one weakness of this system is that web links can become obsolete, or documents may move; more than one version of a document may also be published online.

An alternative system is the use of DOIs (Digital Object Identifiers). These are unique registration codes given to most journal articles published online, which can be used to locate a source more reliably than a URL.

DOIs can be used in a reference in place of a URL.

Example

Burns, N. (2005). Finding Gender. *Politics and Gender*, 1, 137–141. doi:10.1017/S1743923X05221013

Either method, using URL or a DOI, is acceptable.

If you want to use the DOI for a journal article, you can normally locate it on the first page of the document you are using.

2 Using secondary citations

You are reading this text:

Reid, P. (2010). *Gender at Work*. London: Venture Press.

On page 17 of this text you find this paragraph:

> … there is little doubt that the period 1975–2000 saw a substantial increase in jobs held by women in professional fields such as law, medicine, research and management (Mathers, 2003, p.22). However, Webster (2005, p.9) notes that men still tend to occupy more senior positions within professional career fields than their female counterparts.

You wish to include the information from Mathers in your writing, but you haven't actually read it. In this case you have two options: you can find the original text by Mathers and read it, or you can include the information from Mathers using a secondary citation.

How to write a secondary citation

Include the first source (which you have not read) in a citation for the second source (which you have read), using the phrase 'cited in' and a page number.

Examples

According to Mathers (2003, cited in Reid, 2010, p.17), the number of women in professional fields grew between 1975 and 2000.

The years 1975–2000 saw a rise in the number of women in professional fields (Mathers, 2003, cited in Reid, 2010, p.17).

If you want to use a secondary citation, do not include the unread source in your reference list; this should only contain sources which you have actually read.

2a Work in pairs. Discuss which source in the example above should be included in your reference list.

2b Read each of these short texts, then write a paraphrase of the information, and include a correct secondary citation for each one.

Example

Source: Maxwell, 2009, p.117

There is evidence that teenage and adult females have a greater sensitivity to sweet tastes than males do, which may be explained by women having a proportionally greater number of taste buds than men (Hope, 2006).

Requirement	Should	Should not	Reasons
Write in pen	✓		The logbook should be a permanent record.
Write your name and course on the cover of the logbook			
Record the date and experiment title at the beginning of each entry			
Write neatly and clearly while the experiment is going on			
Write rough notes (using symbols and abbreviations) during the experiment and write them up neatly later			
Write in full sentences			
Use a ruler to help you draw any tables or graphs			
Try to 'fix' strange results so they match what you expected			
Change information which seems wrong after you have written it			
Copy information directly from a lab manual into a logbook			
Cross out information			
Add notes, comments and questions that you might think of during the experiment			
Write down any unexpected or apparently incorrect results			
Tear pages out, or glue in pages from other places			

3d Logbooks may include these sections. Work in small groups to decide the best order for this information. Check your answers with another group when you finish.

Method and materials   Theoretical background   Results/observations   Questions

Sources of error   Introduction   Conclusion   Discussion

3e You are going to read about an experiment investigating the sense of taste. Before you begin, discuss these questions in small groups.

1   Do people vary in their ability to sense different tastes?

2   Do you think there is a difference between men's and women's abilities to sense tastes?

3f Read the introduction to an experiment to test whether your sensitivity to sweet tastes is affected by your gender and check your answers to 3e.

Taste sensitivity experiment

Objective

To measure the sugar taste threshold for adults of different sexes.

To determine whether gender affects the ability to taste sugar.

Introduction

There is variation between individuals in their ability to experience different tastes; this may be explained by differing densities of taste buds on the tongue. Despite claims that women have more taste buds than men, studies suggest that taste bud densities do not differ significantly between adults of different sexes (Miller, 1988). Therefore, in an experiment to test whether women are more sensitive to sweet tastes than men, we would expect to see no difference between male and female test subjects.

The biology of taste

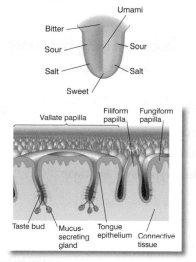

Most humans are able to detect five classes of taste: sweet, sour, bitter, salty, and umami (the taste of amino acids) (Jacob, 2002, p.319). Taste is perceived through taste cells. Taste buds are clusters of taste receptor cells mainly located on the tongue, though some taste buds are also found on the roof of the mouth and the throat. The taste buds themselves are found on special structures called papillae – these are the small pinkish bumps which can be seen on the tip of the tongue. It has been noted that people with more papillae are more sensitive to tastes. The taste threshold is the lowest concentration at which an individual can detect a particular taste.

Hypothesis

There is no gender difference in the sugar taste threshold.

Equipment

1 Sugar
2 Ordinary tap water
3 Five one-litre bottles
4 A digital scale
5 Funnel
6 Small plastic cups with a fill line marked at 40ml

Experiment procedure

This procedure is carried out with five male and five female test subjects.

Preparation:

1 Fill each bottle with exactly 1 litre of water.
2 Dissolve 18g of sugar in the first bottle.
3 Dissolve 9g of sugar in the second bottle.
4 Dissolve 4.5g of sugar in the third bottle.
5 Dissolve 2.25g of sugar in the fourth bottle.
6 Fill the fifth bottle with ordinary tap water.
7 Arrange a set of five plastic cups for each test subject. Each cup should be marked to show the solution that it will hold, in a way that the test subject cannot identify.

Procedure for each test subject:

8 Fill five cups with one of each of the four solutions and one with the tap water, to the 40ml line.
9 Arrange the cups in order from lowest sugar concentration to highest.
10 Ask the test subject to drink from the first cup, and indicate whether they can detect sugar in the solution.
11 The subject takes a drink of distilled water to cleanse the palate.
12 Repeat steps 10 and 11 for each of the five cups.

References

Jacob, T. (2002). The gustatory sensory system. In D. Roberts (Ed.), *Signals and Perception: The fundamentals of human sensation* (pp. 319–330). Basingstoke: Palgrave Macmillan.

Miller, I.J. (1988). Human taste bud densities across adult age groups, *Journal of Gerontology, 43*(1), M26–M30. doi:10.1093/geronj/43.1.M26

3j Work in small groups.

    1 Compare your results. Do not alter any of the results.

    2 Calculate average scores for the male group and female group.

    3 Discuss these points, and make extra notes in your logbook if you need to.

        a Do you have any particular questions or comments about what you observed in the experiment?

        b Did you notice, or think of, any other particular sources of error?

    4 To what extent does the data appear to support the hypothesis?

> **UNIT TASK** **The gender gap**

Later in this unit, you will discuss the topic of the gender gap with your classmates and then write a short overview of the issues involved in your chosen gender gap assignment title. By now you have received some information and data from listening (Unit Task Part A), as well as the two readings (Unit Task Part B). However, your understanding of the topic, and your writing, will be stronger if you can find other sources of information and data.

a Listed below are the bibliographic details of several different sources on the gender gap topic. What type of source (e.g. book, journal, etc.) is each of these?

  1 Authors: Barbara F. Reskin and Denise D. Bielby
            Title: A sociological perspective on gender and career outcomes.
            Journal title: Journal of Economic Perspectives.
            Year of publication: 2005
            Volume number: 19 (Issue 1)
            Pages: 71–86

  2 Authors: Ricardo Hausmann, Laura D. Tyson and Saadia Zahidi
            Title: The Global Gender Gap Report 2009.
            Year of publication: 2009
            Place of publication: Geneva
            Publisher: World Economic Forum

  3 Authors: Francine D. Blau and Lawrence M. Kahn
            Title: The gender pay gap: going, going … but not gone.
            (Appeared as a chapter in a book titled
              'The Declining Significance of Gender')
            Editors: Francine D. Blau, Mary C. Brinton and David B. Grusky
            Year of publication: 2006
            Place of publication: New York
            Publisher: Russell Sage Foundation
            Pages: 37–66

  4 Author: European Commission
            Title: She Figures 2009: Statistics and indicators on gender equality in science.
            Year of publication: 2009
            Place of publication: European Commission
            Place of publication: Brussels
            DOI: 10.2777/10329
            URL: http://ec.europa.eu/research/science-society

5 Authors: Irene Padavic and Barbara Reskin
Title: Women and men at work. (2nd Edition)
Year of publication: 2002
Place of publication: Thousand Oaks
Publisher: Sage

b Use the bibliographic information above to practise writing a reference list which includes each of the sources. (You may decide not to use all of these sources in your writing assignment for this unit, but practising writing these as references now will help you build your skill in this area, and will save you time later.)

c Some of the sources given above are available electronically, while others are print sources. Before the next lesson, do the following:

1 Try to find as many of these sources as you can, either online or in your university library.

2 Try to find some alternative sources by yourself, which you can add to the list.

3 When you find any possible sources, skim read them to decide if they are relevant to the assignment title that you are writing. If you decide that they are relevant, read them and take notes. After you have finished your notes, review the information on the topic from all of the sources which you have found. Use these questions to help you:

a Which of the sources offer similar ideas?

b Are there any sources which offer ideas that are very different from the others?

c What patterns or trends can you see in the data presented by the different sources?

d Is there any information or data which appears to go against the pattern?

 Go to the checklist on p.241. Look again at the tips relating to Unit 1 Parts A–B and tick (✓) those you have used in your studies. Read the tips relating to Unit 1 Part C.

Reporting in speech

By the end of Part D you will be able to:

- discuss the meaning and implications of numerical data
- use statistical data in support of claims
- refer to graphics in support of claims.

1 Discussing the meaning and implications of numerical data

> Discussions are an important part of most areas of UK higher education. The ability to discuss your ideas and support them with data from research is important for your contribution to seminars, your ability to critically evaluate information, and for the development of your knowledge of a topic.

1a Look at the data below about women in the workforce. Work in pairs and discuss your answers to these questions.

1 What does the data in the bar charts (Figures 13 and 14) suggest about the gender gap at work overall?

2 What conclusions can we draw from this information about the gender gap in senior management?

3 What can we conclude about Scandinavian countries from this data?

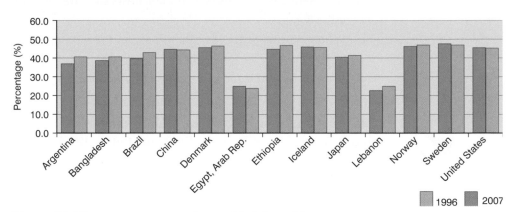

Figure 13: Women as a percentage of total workforce

Source: World Bank, World Development Indicators 2010

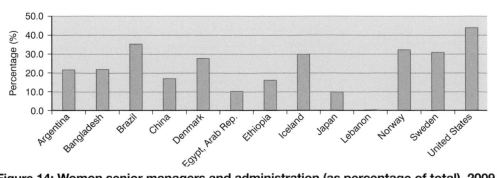

Figure 14: Women senior managers and administration (as percentage of total), 2009

Source: World Bank, 2010

1b You are going to take part in a small group discussion with your classmates on this question.

To what extent is the gender gap narrowing around the world? How can we decide if the gender gap is becoming narrower?

Work in pairs. Each pair should choose one of the sets of data below to use in the discussion. Look at your data and spend a few minutes deciding how it relates to the question above. Discuss your ideas.

Dataset A

1   From the World Economic Forum's 2009 'Global Gender Gap Report'. This measures equality between the sexes from a score of 0.0, indicating complete inequality, to 1.0, indicating complete equality.

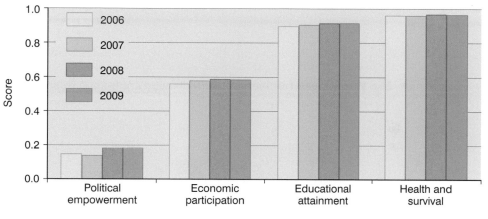

Source: WEF, 2009

2   Percentage of seats held in parliament by women, for selected countries

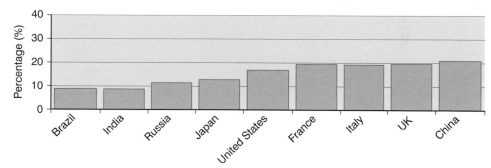

Source: UNDP, Human Development Report, 2009

Dataset B

1 Expected years of schooling, by year, region and gender

Region	Year 2000		2006	
	Male	Female	Male	Female
High income countries	15.1	15.5	15.3	16.0
Middle income countries	10.3	9.4	11.1	10.6
Low income countries	8.3	7.0	9.0	7.7

Source: World Bank, World Development Indicators, 2010

2 Percentage of university students who are female in selected OECD countries, by year

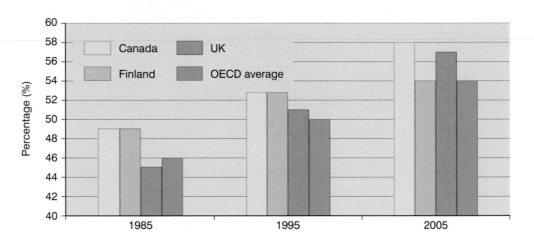

Source: OECD, 2008

Dataset C

1 Women's salaries as a percentage of men's salaries, by year and country

Year / Country	2007 (%)	2009 (%)
Brazil	57	56
Russia	62	63
China	64	65
Mozambique	81	81
Japan	44	46
USA	62	64
Chile	39	41
Vietnam	71	71

Source: World Economic Forum, Global Gender Gap Report 2007, 2009

2 Female professional and technical workers (as percentage of total workforce for that sector)

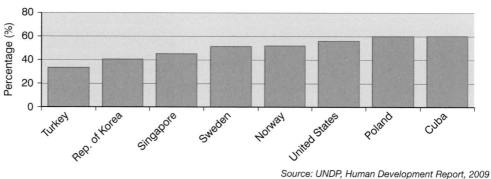

Source: UNDP, Human Development Report, 2009

1c Work in groups of three, so that each student has looked at a different set of data. Take turns giving a verbal summary of the data that you looked at for the other members of your group. Complete the table below as you listen.

Dataset	Main trends	Significant information
A		
B		
C		

1d Imagine that your group is going to give a presentation on the question in 1b. You must prepare a response to the question which all of your group members accept. Discuss the question together to find a single position on the topic which all members of your group agree with.

2 Using statistical data in support of claims

> Statistical data helps to support the ideas that you present, demonstrating that your ideas are based on evidence from reliable research and making your work more credible.

2a Work in small groups. Brainstorm reasons why women's earnings over the course of a working lifetime tend to be lower than men's.

2b Discuss these questions with your group.

   1 To what extent are women's lower lifetime earnings the result of discrimination only?

   2 What is the relationship between motherhood and lifetime earnings?

   3 What is the relationship between education, job type and lifetime earnings?

2c Look at the UK data in Figures 15, 16 and 17 below. Identify data which you think could further support your opinions.

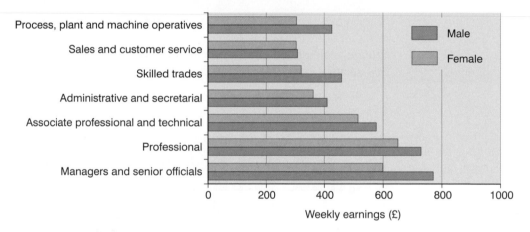

Source: ONS, Annual Survey of Hours and Earnings, 2009

Figure 15: Gross weekly earnings by occupation

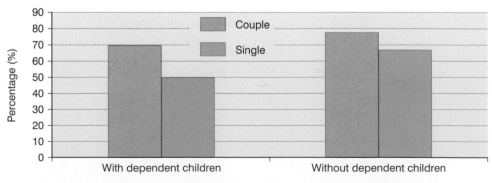

Source: DWP, Labour Market Trends, 2002

Figure 16: Employment rates for partnered and single women with and without dependent children; United Kingdom; spring 2002, not seasonally adjusted

Sex \ Year	2000	2005	2006	2007	2008
Male	78.94	78.77	78.38	78.44	78.54
Female	65.55	66.69	66.84	66.31	66.87

Source: OECD Stat Extract, 2010

Figure 17: Share of each gender of working age in employment

2d These data sources are all based on the UK. In your groups, discuss the extent to which you think they can be generalized to describe the situation in other countries.

2e Discuss this topic in small groups. During the discussion, introduce your own claims and support them with data.

What explanation is there for the fact that women often have lower earnings than men?

3 Referring to graphics in support of claims

Audiences can often appreciate statistical data more easily when the speaker presents it to them as a graphic, rather than simply presenting the data orally.

The following points are important to bear in mind when deciding whether to present data in graphic form:

- Does the presentation of data in a graphic help to support a specific claim?
- Will the graphic help the audience to analyze the data?
- Will the graphic help to communicate a pattern, trend or main idea to the audience?

References to a graphic in speech frequently follow a sequence similar to the one below:

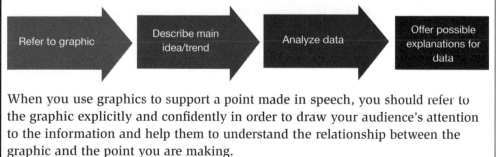

When you use graphics to support a point made in speech, you should refer to the graphic explicitly and confidently in order to draw your audience's attention to the information and help them to understand the relationship between the graphic and the point you are making.

3a Work in pairs. Think of phrases that you can use to draw your audience's attention to a graphic. Make a note of your ideas on p.46 then compare your answers with another pair of students.

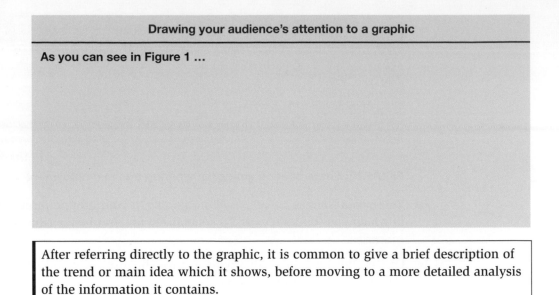

Drawing your audience's attention to a graphic

As you can see in Figure 1 …

> After referring directly to the graphic, it is common to give a brief description of the trend or main idea which it shows, before moving to a more detailed analysis of the information it contains.

3b Look at these graphics. Work in pairs. How would you describe the main trend in each graphic?

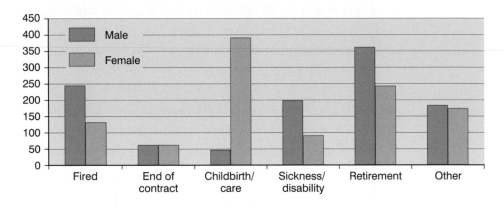

Source: Unpublished survey of 1,100 workers aged 15–65

Figure 18: Reasons for leaving previous job

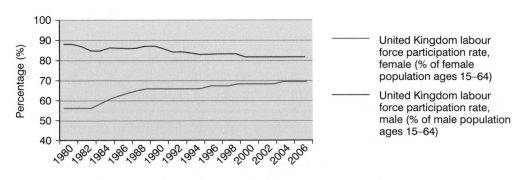

Source: World Bank, World Development Indicators, 2009

Figure 19: UK labour force participation rates

You should not simply give a word-for-word description of data in the graphic which your audience can already see for themselves. Expressions of statistics can often be replaced by more general descriptions in speech. For instance, this can be done by:

- only describing minimum values, maximum values or averages
- describing numerical values as proportions.

3c Use either of these two methods to practise describing the graphics above to your partner.

It is important to give comments on, or possible explanations for, the data that you are describing. Look at these phrases, which can be used for this purpose. Note that you do not need to be certain of the reasons, as you are only suggesting possibilities.

Phrases for explaining and commenting on data

A possible explanation for this is …

This may be explained by the fact that …

This data may be due to …

This [change] may be attributable to …

It may be that this is due to …

This suggests that …

It seems from this that …

What this shows is …

3d Look again at the graphics in 3b (Figures 18 and 19). Work in pairs. Each pair should choose one graphic and take a few minutes to prepare a short report about the data in the graphic. Remember that you need to give a brief introduction, refer to the graphic, briefly describe the main idea of the graphic, then offer possible explanations for – or comments on – the data.

3e Work with another student who chose a different graphic. Take turns presenting your report to your partner. As you listen to your partner, decide whether you agree with their possible explanation for the data.

3f Work in small groups to complete this table. Use the questions below to help you think of the different strengths and weaknesses of these common ways to represent data.

1 What types of data can be represented best by each graphic?
2 What types of data is each graphic unsuitable for?

Reporting in writing

By the end of Part E you will be able to:

- identify different types of report
- understand the core features of a typical written report
- write a literature review
- build paragraphs in academic writing
- create a poster to report results.

1 Identifying different types of report

1a Work in small groups. Discuss whether any reports are written in your subject field. If so, what types of report are common?

1b Look at this table and match the report types (1–5) with the definitions (a–e).

Report type	Definition
1 Lab report	a A report which presents an overview of the latest developments in a situation. It explains the development of a project, problems which have been encountered, and outlines how the project is expected to go from here.
2 General research report	b A large piece of paper which presents a piece of research.
3 Feasibility/recommendation report	c A written report which presents the results of a piece of scientific research, for instance an experiment.
4 Progress report	d A report written to compare options, or assess whether a proposed activity is possible.
5 Poster	e A report outlining key information on a broad topic. This could be new research data gathered by the author through fieldwork, or it may be a report based on research data from other written sources.

2 Understanding the core features of a typical written report

> A lot of writing in higher education can be divided into essays and reports. Essays and reports tend to differ in their layout, the types of purpose for which they are written, and, to an extent, the language they use.

2a Work in pairs to decide which of these features are more characteristic of essays (E) and which are more characteristic of reports (R). Some answers may be applicable to both types of writing.

1 Structures information using contents pages, headings, subheadings, etc.

2 Makes an original argument

3 Attempts to find solutions for a specific problem

4 Explores ideas on a topic

5 Collates available data on a subject

6   Attempts to define the parameters of a particular problem

7   Evaluates data and makes a recommendation

8   Presents the results of a piece of empirical research

9   Develops an idea through argument

10   May be personal in tone

11   Tends to be impersonal in tone

12   Offers a personal opinion on a topic, then attempts to persuade the reader to accept the opinion

> Typically, essays are more personal expressions of a writer's original ideas. As such, the writer is responsible for structuring the essay so that links between paragraphs and sections are clear in the text, helping the reader to follow the development of the ideas. There are many different ways to structure an essay successfully. Reports are often more formal and impersonal documents, and frequently have a set layout. They tend to have a clear division of the main body into sections and subsections, and may use contents pages and numbering systems to help make the structure of the report clear.

2b   Work in small groups to decide the sequence of sections which are commonly found in a report.

Conclusion   *7*

Discussion of findings   *6*

References   *8*

Appendices   *9*

Method and materials (or approach) used for gathering data   *4*

Title page   1

Introduction   *3*

Abstract   *2*

Results (findings)   *5*

2c   The report sections in 2b are very common to many report types. However, some report types differ from this. Work in pairs. Match the report types (1–3) with the three typical report outlines (a–c).

1   Feasibility/recommendation report

2   Progress report

3   Lab report

a

Introduction
Objective
Theoretical background
Materials and methods   *lab*
Results
Discussion
Conclusions
References

b

Introduction
Background
Presentation of option(s)
Requirements
Evaluation of option(s)
Conclusions
Recommendations
References

recon

c

Introduction
How much has been completed
What is currently being done
What remains to be done
Problems encountered
Summary of status
Points of interest which have emerged from the project
Conclusion

Progress

2d The sequence in which these parts appear can vary. Work in three groups. Each group should consider one of the report outlines above. To what extent can the order of sections be changed?

2e In your groups, explain your ideas about ordering the parts of a report to the class. Give reasons for your opinions.

3 Writing a literature review

Literature reviews are pieces of writing which summarize the current state of knowledge on a particular topic. They usually appear in lab reports, research proposals, dissertations and academic research reports, or are sometimes published on their own in order to collate current information on a topic. A literature review can have several purposes:

- to summarize existing information on the topic
- to compare and synthesize information from different sources
- to show your interpretation of these sources and give an idea of how your research will contribute to the existing information
- to show that your own writing will be based on suitable academic sources
- to show how your own study is a valuable contribution to the academic community's knowledge of the topic that you are studying.

Common features of a literature review include:

1 Definition and discussion of key terms.

2 An explanation of why the topic is important.

3 Identification of key problems or questions.

4 Description of different solutions or approaches to answering the key questions that have been offered by other writers. This should also include:

    a your comments about the extent to which you accept the claims and ideas of other writers

    b any limitations of the writers' studies which may make their conclusions less valid.

5 A conclusion which summarizes the main points of the literature review and shows how your own study will contribute to the research which has already been done.

3a Look at the example literature review, which comes from an academic research report focusing on job satisfaction among young female workers in the UK. Underline any of the features 1–5 above that you find, and make a note of the feature in the margin.

Literature review

Job satisfaction can be defined as a worker's subjective assessment of their happiness with the work they do. An understanding of what factors influence job satisfaction is critical for two reasons. Firstly, it can guide policy makers and those involved in the campaign for better working conditions, but also because higher job satisfaction is likely to lead to better work performance and lower turnover costs for employers.

Clark and Oswald (1996) were the first to create a model of the factors involved in job satisfaction. They drew a link between earned income and satisfaction, but also introduced the importance of expectations: greater job satisfaction is found where the gap between actual and expected wages is small. Clark and Oswald therefore claimed that the amount of money earned is not, by itself, the most important element of job satisfaction. This has become particularly significant in the debate about the sources of women's satisfaction at work, and explanations for the so-called gender / job satisfaction paradox.

It is widely accepted that women tend to have greater job satisfaction than men. This is often explained in part as being due to women having low expectations of what they will be able to earn, or how likely they are to be promoted. If women do not have such high expectations of salary or career advancement as men do, then it follows that they will be more satisfied with less attractive earnings and career outcomes. However, as Hammermesh (2000) notes, job expectations and actual work experiences change during the course of a career, and so it is unlikely that male and female expectations are uniformly different. This would seem to undermine Clark and Oswald's claim for low expectations, though findings from a large body of studies following Clark suggest that it is at least part of the reason.

Quite separately from the issue of low expectations, Clark and Oswald (ibid) suggest that another possible reason for women's higher job satisfaction despite lower earnings is because men and women value specific aspects of their work, such as pay or flexible work arrangements, differently (Clark, 1997). However, it is again unlikely that this is sufficient explanation for the gender satisfaction gap, and may even underestimate the importance of the similarities between the genders. In a study of job attitudes among US lawyers, Mueller and Wallace (1996) find that the perception of fair pay between male and female workers is a significant element of female job satisfaction.

Furthermore, women's work experience levels are not uniform; for instance, younger female workers tend to have work experiences and expectations which are similar to male colleagues of the same age. This is particularly evident among workers in professional jobs and with higher education (Royalty, 1998), which would seem to be supported by the findings of Mueller and Wallace (ibid). It therefore seems that different job expectations cannot account fully for the gender / job satisfaction difference.

In conclusion, there is widespread agreement that a gender / job satisfaction gap does exist. Following early studies by Clark and others (see, for example, Hodson, 1989) it has long been assumed that this is a result of male and female workers having different expectations of their career success, or indeed having significantly different opinions about what aspects of a job are important for a feeling of contentment. However, these theories are challenged by studies which show that levels of expectation differ between women of different age, occupational type and educational level. While most studies of age-dependent differences of expectations have been carried out in the United States, little has yet been done to investigate whether this is true in the UK. The aim of the present study, therefore, is to explore in more detail whether young female workers in the UK share career progress expectations with their male colleagues.

3b Compare your answers with a partner.

3c Two common ways of structuring a literature review are *chronological* and *topical*. Read the description of each structure below. Work in pairs. Discuss which structure has been used for the literature review above.

Chronological structure

This can be used to show the development of research on a topic over time, and how ideas have changed.

Introduction

+

Paragraph 1 – Describe earliest study and key ideas or methods established by this study.

+

Paragraph 2 – Next study: describe any similarities or differences in ideas, methods or findings between this study and the first one.

+

Paragraph 3 – Next study: describe any similarities or differences in ideas, methods or findings between this study and the previous ones.

+

Concluding paragraph – Summarize main points of literature and explain how your own study fits into the literature.

Structured by topic

This can be used to compare different authors' ideas about different aspects of the topic, as well as their claims and methods.

Introduction

+

Paragraph 1 – Describe key topic and compare different opinions and findings on this topic from different authors.

+

Paragraph 2 – Next topic: briefly introduce issue and compare different opinions and findings on this topic from different authors.

+

Paragraph 3 – Next topic: briefly introduce issue and compare different opinions and findings on this topic from different authors.

+

Concluding paragraph – Summarize main points of literature and explain how your own study fits into the literature.

3d Imagine that you are writing a study about the reasons why women seem to have greater job satisfaction than men. You have found four sources while reading through the literature on this topic. These are summarized below. Read the sources and answer these questions.

   a Which ones deal with these topics?

- Occupational type and job satisfaction
- Female-dominated workplaces
- Ideas or expectations about men's and women's work

   b Which of the sources make similar claims?

   c Do any of the sources offer conflicting claims or information?

A

Clark, A. (1997). Why are women so happy at work? *Labour Economics, 4,* pp.341–372.

Clark reports on the results of a survey of attitudes to work in Britain, with information on job satisfaction gathered from about 2,500 adults. Clark finds that women overall report significantly higher levels of job satisfaction than men do, but claims that the gender difference in job satisfaction levels is not caused by different types of work, or different ideas about work value. Clark explains the gender difference in job satisfaction as resulting from the fact that women expect different things from their work than men do, and that women's jobs more closely match their expectations than men's do. Clark claims that women have lower expectations of their jobs than men. Clark also claims there is less of a gender / job satisfaction difference between young workers, people in professional fields, and those who work in male-dominated workplaces.

B

Sousa-Poza, A., & Sousa-Poza, A.A. (2000). Taking another look at the gender / job satisfaction paradox. *Kyklos*, *53*(2), pp.135–152.

The authors question why women earn lower wages than men, face more discrimination at work, and find it more difficult to be promoted than men do, but have higher levels of job satisfaction. The authors claim that differences in job satisfaction levels are the result of different ideas about levels of education, number of working hours, job security, promotion opportunities, salary, being able to help others, good relations between workers and management.

Their study analyzes data from 21 countries around the world, giving information for 15,324 workers. The authors also claim that large differences in job satisfaction are seen mainly in the USA and UK, and do not apply to all other countries surveyed. Countries such as Germany, the Netherlands and Russia showed almost no difference in job satisfaction between the genders, and women tended to have lower job satisfaction than men in Japan, France, Cyprus and Spain. The authors suggest that women in the USA and UK have higher job satisfaction because women in these countries put more emphasis on job security, good relationships with co-workers and being able to do meaningful work than men.

C

Donohue, S.M., & Heywood, J.S. (2004). Job satisfaction and gender: an expanded specification from the NLSY. *International Journal of Manpower*, *25*(2), pp.211–234.

Donohue and Heywood analyzed results from the US National Longitudinal Survey of Youth, with a sample size of 12,686 individuals. They found that there is no general gender / job satisfaction gap between young men and women. However, they did discover there are gender / job satisfaction differences depending on occupation type: blue-collar males have higher job satisfaction than blue-collar females, while white-collar females report higher satisfaction than white-collar males. They also found that women's reasons for their job satisfaction differ from men. For male workers, job satisfaction depends more on status and higher earnings; for female workers, job satisfaction is less closely connected to earnings, and depends more on fringe benefits such as childcare or flexible working hours.

D

Bender, K.A., Donohue, S.M., & Heywood, J. S. (2005). Job satisfaction and gender segregation. *Oxford Economic Papers*, *57*, pp.479–496.

Bender et al. note that women have higher levels of job satisfaction than men, despite having lower wages and less chance of being promoted within their careers. The authors focus on data for 1,854 people from the 1997 National Study of the Changing Workforce in the USA. They find that the main explanation for women's higher job satisfaction is that women do not think salary is as important as men do; instead, the authors claim that women put more value on workplaces which allow them to work flexibly to be able to balance their work and home life. They claim that women who work in female-dominated workplaces have the highest job satisfaction, because these workplaces also tend to offer more flexibility in work arrangements. Therefore, women are more satisfied at work because they tend to choose workplaces where their satisfaction will be highest.

3e Write a short literature review using the information you have found in the four sources. Remember that you should write in your own words and avoid copying phrases from the summaries. You may find it helpful to refer back to the advice about paraphrasing in SS1 Unit 2 Part E.

4 Building paragraphs in academic writing

To be effective, a report needs to include the following:

- a clear structure divided into sections with headings
- a logical development of ideas in each section and between sections
- paragraphs which show a logical progression of ideas and which are clearly linked to other paragraphs in the same section (and the overall structure of the whole piece of work).

Linking ideas between paragraphs

By showing how different paragraphs link together, the writer can help the audience to understand the development of ideas in the work more easily.

4a Look at the following short excerpt from an academic essay. The writer has not made the links between the paragraphs very clear. Work in pairs. Write a linking sentence on the line that will help to make the ideas in paragraph 1 flow into paragraph 2.

> The mass entry of women into the workforce has been one of the greatest social changes in the UK since the mid-20th century. This has resulted in changes in the character of the workforce and expected working conditions. Social norms are also changing. Marriage and childbearing are occurring later, divorce rates are rising and there are even changes in the very structure of family life: more working women are now comfortable living as single parents, and in an increasing number of cases working as the family breadwinner while the male partner takes the role of 'househusband'.
>
> _____
>
> Women now make up just under 60% of all UK university students. Though the number of female students has been increasing steadily for some time now, it is still a major change from earlier decades (in the 1970s, for instance, women accounted for less than half of all UK university graduates). There have also been consistent increases in the number of female students enrolling on formerly 'male' courses such as engineering and the natural sciences.

4b Compare your ideas with another pair of students. Are there any differences in the methods you have chosen to make the links?

4c Work in pairs. Read this paragraph, which comes from the main body of a report about differences in men's and women's job satisfaction at work. Try to guess the topic of the paragraph that preceded this one. What topic is likely to follow in the next paragraph? How do you know?

Age can also impact relative satisfaction levels, though not nearly as much as education. Younger female workers in the 25–34 age group showed the least dissimilarity to male colleagues in the same age group (only a 3% gap), while in the 55+ group the difference in satisfaction had climbed to 7%. This lends weight to arguments that more women are entering the workforce in traditionally male-dominated occupations. However, both education and age are fairly minor contributors to a sense of job satisfaction compared to concerns about fair wages.

Using specific features to build paragraphs

4d Look at the list of common possible features of a paragraph below. Read the example paragraph below and work in pairs to identify the features that you find.

1 A link to a previous paragraph

2 A topic sentence

3 A more detailed explanation of the topic sentence

4 Supporting information

5 Comments about the meaning or implications of the supporting information

6 A link to the next paragraph

Another possible reason for the rise in women's participation in the workforce has been the reduction of discrimination in the workplace. Women in the OECD nations today benefit from greatly reduced sexual discrimination at work, which has encouraged increasing numbers of women to seek professional careers, a situation which differs markedly from the first half of the 20th century. For instance, according to Vincent-Lancrin (2008, p.279), between the years 1900 and 1950, women in the USA were barred from half of all jobs. The USA is by no means the only example of this sort, and it is likely that similar statistics can be produced for almost all other nations until the very recent past. Changing attitudes to women's roles in society mean that, even if full equality has not been reached, it is now easier than ever for women to participate in the workforce in a range of careers, though discrimination does still exist in some areas.

4e Review the information you have gathered about the gender gap throughout this unit. Choose one of the questions below, which you will write a short essay on (consisting of an introduction and conclusion, as well as two or three main body paragraphs).

1 In what ways can the gender gap be measured?

2 What are the possible explanations for the gender gap in salaries?

3 How has the gender gap situation changed in recent decades?

4f After you choose a question, review the information about the gender gap that you have learned in Unit 1. What information will you include?

4g Plan and write the essay. Try to build your paragraphs in the ways suggested above, and use clear links to show how the paragraphs are related to each other.

5 Creating a poster to report results

Posters are used in a number of different academic fields, particularly in the natural sciences and engineering, to present the results of research. Posters are usually presented at conferences. During a poster presentation session, the researcher stands by their poster to talk about their research and answer questions from conference delegates. Poster presentation sessions are a convenient way to learn more about the most up-to-date research activity in your field. They also provide an opportunity to make useful contacts. Posters often follow the order of sections in a primary research report. Typical sections in a science or engineering poster include:

1 Introduction
2 Methods
3 Results
4 Conclusions
5 References
6 Acknowledgements

5a Work in pairs. Think about the needs of the audience/reader at a poster presentation and then tick (✓) which of these statements about posters meet the audience's needs best. Be prepared to explain your reasons.

1 The introduction of the poster should help the audience to understand the topic and aim of your research as quickly as possible.

2 The introduction should give a very detailed overview of the topic and previous research.

3 The font size of the poster should be as small as possible, to allow you to put more detail on the poster.

4 The poster should present information concisely, in a way which is easy for a viewer to read and understand quickly.

5 The poster should include as many colourful decorations and pictures as possible, in order to attract viewers.

6 The poster should be written in long sentences to explain ideas in detail, just like an essay.

7 You should use every possible bit of space on the poster, in order to get as much detail into the space as possible.

8 The poster should contain as much detail as possible, so that the reader can get a full understanding of the research.

9 The poster should present key information in graphic form, which is easy for the viewer to understand.

10 The poster should 'stand alone' – a viewer should be able to read and understand it without too much verbal explanation from the researcher.

5b Discuss your ideas in small groups. Explain your reasons for the answers you have given.

4   Can each section be read and understood easily?

5   Is the flow of information clear and easy to follow?

6   Is everything on the poster relevant and necessary?

7   Is the font size large enough?

8   Is the amount of text suitable?

9   Is the amount of information presented graphically suitable?

10 Is the amount of white space suitable?

Poster 1

Gender differences in the sugar taste threshold
Robert Marshall and Geng Xu

Introduction

An experiment was conducted to investigate whether there was any difference in the ability of adult males and females to taste sugar in solution.

Background

Human taste relies on taste cells on the tongue, clusters of which are known as taste buds (Jacob, 2002). Number of taste buds varies with each individual. Anecdotal evidence suggests females have more taste buds than males, though research indicates this is not the case (Miller, 1988).

Method

Equipment
  Sugar
  Ordinary tap water
  Five 1 litre bottles
  A digital scale
  Funnel
  Small plastic cups

Procedure
Four solutions of sugar in varying concentrations were prepared in marked beakers. A fifth beaker contained tap water without sugar.

Figure 1: Sugar quantities per litre

Phase 1
100 adults (50 male and 50 female) were given a sip of each solution and asked to indicate whether they could detect sugar.
Participants took a sip of clean water between each glass.

Phase 2
Experiment repeated at timed intervals.

Results

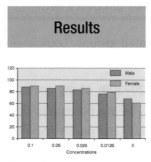

Figure 2: Relative ability to detect sugar

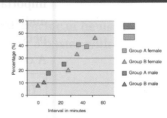

Figure 3: Accuracy of detection increases with longer intervals

Conclusions

No significant differences were found between males' and females' ability to detect sugar. For both sexes, detection rate decreased with lower concentrations.
Time lapse between tastings improved detection rate.

References

Jacob, T. (2002). The gustatory sensory system. In Roberts, D. (Ed.), *Signals and Perception: The fundamentals of human sensation*. Basingstoke: Palgrave Macmillan. (pp. 319–330).

Miller, I.J. (1988). Human taste bud densities across adult age groups. *Journal of Gerontology, 43*(1), M26-M30. doi:10.1093/geronj/43.1.M26

Poster 2

Gender differences in the sugar taste threshold
Robert Marshall and Geng Xu

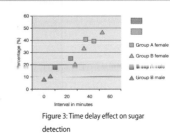

Introduction

Human taste relies on taste cells on the tongue, clusters of which are known as taste buds (Jacob, 2002). The number of taste buds varies with each individual, so it is not certain how many taste buds someone has. Anecdotal evidence suggests females have more taste buds than males, though research indicates this is not the case (Miller, 1988). An experiment was conducted to investigate whether there was any difference in the ability of adult males and females to taste sugar in solution.

Figure 1: A human tongue

Procedure

Four concentrations of sugar were prepared in marked beakers. A fifth beaker contained tap water without sugar.

1. 18 grams
2. 9 grams
3. 4.5 grams
4. 2.25 grams
5. 0 grams

Phase 1

100 adults (50 male and 50 female) were given solutions of sugar and asked to indicate whether they could detect sugar.
Participants took a sip of clean water between each glass.

Phase 2

Experiment repeated at timed intervals.

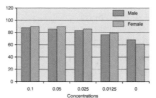

Figure 2: Relative ability to detect sugar

Figure 3: Time delay effect on sugar detection

No significant differences were found between males' and females' ability to detect sugar. For both sexes, detection rate decreased with lower concentrations.
Time lapse between tastings improved detection rate.

References

Jacob, T. (2002). The gustatory sensory system. In Roberts, D. (Ed.), Signals and Perception: The fundamentals of human sensation. Basingstoke: Palgrave Macmillan. (pp. 319–330).

Miller, I.J. (1988). Human taste bud densities across adult age groups. Journal of Gerontology, 43 (1), M26-M30. doi:10.1093/geronj/43.1.M26

Unit 2   Water

Unit overview

Part	This part will help you to ...	By improving your ability to ...
A	**Follow discussions between multiple speakers**	• follow seminar discussions • compare and synthesize ideas and arguments.
B	**Read for a purpose**	• find texts which are at a suitable academic level for your needs • skim read a report to decide if it suits your purpose • understand feasibility/recommendation reports.
C	**Develop your ability to do academic research**	• understand the research process • understand primary and secondary research • analyze the process of choosing a research question • write research proposals.
D	**Participate in group discussions**	• participate in seminar discussions • exchange and challenge ideas appropriately in academic discussion • express and defend opinions • change the direction of a discussion • conclude a discussion.
E	**Write academic reports**	• understand the main features of a primary research report • understand the main features of a successful feasibility/recommendation report • make choices about the best way to structure your reports.

Understanding spoken information

By the end of Part A you will be able to:

- follow seminar discussions
- compare and synthesize ideas and arguments.

1 Following seminar discussions

> Seminar discussions give you the opportunity to compare your ideas with other students and develop your knowledge of a topic. However, it can sometimes be difficult to follow several different people's ideas during a discussion.

1a Work in small groups. Discuss and make a note of strategies that you could use to help you to follow several people's ideas during a discussion.

Strategies to follow discussions
Ask your classmates to repeat anything that you don't understand

2.1

1b Listen to a seminar group discussing strategies that they use. Add any new ideas that you hear to the box.

1c Work in small groups. Discuss which of the strategies in 1a and 1b you have used yourself. Are there any strategies which you find difficult to use? Explain your reasons to your group.

> In *Skills for Study* Level 1 you were introduced to signposting expressions: words and phrases which speakers sometimes use to signal what they are about to say. For instance, a speaker who says 'Can we move on?' is probably about to change the subject that is being discussed, or a speaker who says 'I don't see it like that' is signalling that they disagree with a point that has been made. It can be useful to listen for signposting phrases like this which help you to follow the thread of a discussion more easily.

2.2

1d Listen to three excerpts from the discussion in 1b again. Which of these things does the speaker seem to be doing in each case? (More than one answer is possible for most of the excerpts.)

1 Showing agreement
2 Showing disagreement
3 Adding to a point already made
4 Changing the subject
5 Summarizing/recapping
6 Referring to other sources

1e Work in pairs. Compare your answers. Give reasons for your answers.

1f   Work in small groups. Think of examples of discussion signposts, and make a note of them below.

1 Showing agreement

That's right!

I agree with you.   ~~of james just said~~

That is true

~~I agree~~ of course

2 Showing disagreement

I don't see it like that!

- I disagree / that maybe true / but   to digress a little
- I see your point, but...   building on what Anna just said.
- I see it defferently

3 Adding to a point already made

In addition, ...

as jamse just said

- more over
- on the other hand
- I'd just like to add
- additionaly / building on what Anna just said

4 Changing the subject

Shall we move on?

lets move in

a separate point is

·|

5 Summarizing and recapping

What have we got so far?

to sum

in conclude

OK, lets us mummarize

to recap

6 Referring to other sources

Wallis states that ...

~~in conclude~~

According to

Iam afraid

1g Look at the phrases below, and add them to the correct column in the table in 1f.

a According to Harrison …

ⓑ To recap then, … / Let's recap.

c A separate point is …

d That's true.

e OK, let's just summarize …

f That may be true, but …

g I'd just like to add …

h Another thing is …

ⓘ As James just said …

ⓙ Shall we come back to this later?

k I see it differently.

ⓛ On top of that, …

m To digress a little, …

n Chang showed that …

o So, what we're saying is …

p That's all very well, but …

q Weber claims that …

r Can I raise a different point?

ⓢ Yes, I agree.

ⓣ So, to sum up, ….

u Additionally …

v It's possible I suppose, but …

ⓦ Building on what Anna just said, …

you know
hangeh

1h Work in small groups. You are going to listen to two students discussing the different ways in which water is used as a resource. Before you listen:

1 Brainstorm the different ways humans use water as a resource.

2 Discuss what pressures there are on water supplies.

3 Discuss what it might mean to describe water as 'The issue of the century'.

2.3

1i Listen to the discussion. While you listen, make notes below.

Speaker	Key ideas	Supporting points or evidence
Tony		Needed for drinking and cooking
	Pressure on water supplies is due to overpopulation.	
Liz		e.g. use for hygiene purposes (cleaning, laundry, bathroom, etc.)
	Water is essential not just for domestic use, but in all human activities.	
	Greater industrial development leads to more pressure on water resources.	
	There are direct and indirect pressures on water from overpopulation.	

1j Listen again and tick (✓) any of the phrases in 1g that you hear the speakers use.

2 Comparing and synthesizing ideas and arguments

Comparing information from two or more sources allows you to think more critically and helps to develop your own position on a topic. This means not just listening and taking notes in order to understand what the lecturer is saying, but comparing what they have said with other sources – for instance, a book which you have read on the same topic, or another lecture about the subject which you have listened to. The comparison of information from other sources helps you to develop your own position on a topic, in a process known as *synthesis*.

Ideas of your own + Ideas from first speaker + Ideas from second speaker → Your opinion, based on a comparison of your own and the other speakers' ideas, and any fresh insights of your own

2a Work in pairs. Think of reasons why the ability to synthesize information is a valued skill in higher education.

2b You are going to listen to excerpts from two separate lectures about the problem of global water supply. Before you listen, work in small groups and discuss these questions.

    1 It is often said that there is a global water crisis. What does this mean? Do you agree with this claim?

    2 What activity accounts for most of the water used around the world?

2.4

2c Listen to the excerpt from the first lecture. As you listen, make notes of some of the main ideas.

Lecture 1	
Issue	**Main ideas/evidence**
The potential shortage of water available in the world	
The reasons why the world's supply of fresh water is put under pressure	

2d Listen again. Add information or evidence that the speaker gives to support their claims.

2e Work in small groups and compare your notes. Discuss these questions.

    1 Do you have the same information?

    2 To what extent do you agree or disagree with the points made in the lecture? Give reasons for your opinions.

2.5

2f Listen to the excerpt from the second lecture. As you listen, make notes of some of the main ideas.

Lecture 2	
Issue	Main ideas/evidence
The potential shortage of water available in the world	
The reasons why the world's supply of fresh water is put under pressure	

2g Work in small groups and compare your notes. Find two things which both speakers seem to agree on.

> Both speakers mention that only about 20–25% of the total fresh water in the world is in use by humans. This is a fact – it can be researched and verified easily, and few people claim that this is untrue. However, the two speakers make different comments about this fact:
>
> **Speaker 1** This is a relatively small amount of water.
>
> **Speaker 2** This is more than enough water for the human population's needs.
>
> These are interpretations of the fact: they may or may not be accurate.

2.4 & 2.5

2h Both speakers agree that the world's water resources are under strain. However, they have differing interpretations of the seriousness of this information. Look at the information given by the two speakers in the first column of the table on p.72. Listen again. For each piece of information, decide which of the two interpretations the speakers give.

Type of water source	Problems	Benefits

Assignment 2

In this unit task you will complete a number of activities centred around an experiment to determine the refractive index of water.

a   In this section of the unit task, you will watch a video of someone conducting the experiment. Before you watch, read the text below and answer these questions.

  1   What happens when light is 'refracted'?

  2   What causes light beams to refract?

  3   What happens to the appearance of an object when it is viewed in water?

  4   What is the difference between the 'real depth' of an object in water and its 'apparent depth'?

http://vimeo.
com/14854730

b   While you watch:

  1   Make notes about the basic procedure.

  2   Write down any questions about the experiment that occur to you while you are watching it.

c   Work in small groups. Discuss your questions. Ask your group members or teacher to clarify any points that you are unsure of.

Determining the refractive index of water

Objectives

1   To measure the refractive index of water as a ratio of real depth to apparent depth.

2   To determine whether the refractive index of water is affected by salinity.

Introduction and theory

The speed at which light travels varies depending on the substances through which it is passing; light travels more slowly when it passes through a denser substance. Refraction occurs when the direction in which light is moving changes as it passes at an oblique angle from one substance (medium) to another of a different density (for instance, between water and air, or air and glass). This is caused by a change in the speed of light as it passes across the boundary between the two media.

Different substances have a different characteristic refractive index (RI), which is the extent to which that substance will cause light to refract as it passes through it.

Angles of refraction are measured as the incident angle, and the refraction angle. In Snell's Law, the refractive index (RI) of a medium can be measured as

$$\frac{Sin\ i}{Sin\ r} = n \quad \text{where:}$$

i is the angle of incidence

r is the angle of refraction

n is the refractive index

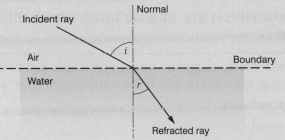

Figure 1: Refraction of light passing between two substances

The refractive index for a given medium at a given temperature is a constant.

Determining the refractive index of water

Where the line of view is perpendicular to the surface of the water, the refractive index of water (n) can be measured as $\frac{RD}{AD} = n$

RD is the real depth

AD is the apparent depth

Real depth

This is the actual depth, in centimetres, of the water.

Apparent depth

Refraction makes an object in water appear to be in a different position.

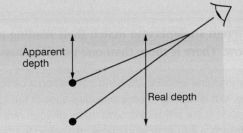

Figure 2: Differences in real and apparent depth caused by refraction

Apparent depth can be measured by knowing that any object held above a mirror appears to be an equal distance behind the mirror. The apparent depth of a pin at the bottom of a container filled with water can be measured if the height of a second pin above the surface is adjusted so that its reflection in a mirror looks exactly the same as the refracted image of the first pin.

Therefore, apparent depth can be measured as the distance in centimetres from the second pin to the top surface of the water.

Go to the checklist on p.241 and read the tips relating to Unit 2 Part A.

1e Read the texts again and underline any words or phrases you don't understand.

1f Work in pairs. Compare what you've underlined. Discuss which text was easier to understand. Give reasons for your answer.

1g Search in your university library catalogue for different types of text on the subject you are studying. In particular, identify:

- any introductory-level textbooks
- a subject-specific dictionary (e.g. A Dictionary of Sociology).

2 Skim reading a report to decide if it suits your purpose

The formal structure and layout of reports make it easy for a reader to skim read them to get a general understanding of their content. Students who are busy with research do not have time to read through every possible source carefully before deciding if it is useful or not. Looking at the features below can help you decide if a text is likely to contain the information that you need.

- abstract
- introduction
- headings
- subheadings
- captions
- graphics
- tables
- conclusion
- key words

2a Skim read the report in **Appendix 3**. Look only at the features identified in the information box above. Take notes in the second column of the table below.

Questions	Notes
What is the main idea of this text?	
What aspects of the topic does the author consider?	
What supporting evidence does the author give?	
What recommendations does the author make?	

2b Work in pairs and compare your notes.

2c Decide how useful the report in **Appendix 3** would be for each of these assignment titles.

    1 You are writing an essay with this title:

       Discuss the causes and effects of poverty in developing nations.

    2 You are writing a report with this title:

       Outline the social effects of lack of water.

    3 You are writing a report with this title:

       Describe and evaluate different water supply technologies.

    4 You are writing a report with this title:

       Examine the impact of water shortage in sub-Saharan Africa.

2d Imagine that you are writing assignment 2 in 2c. Read through the report in **Appendix 3** carefully and take detailed notes of relevant information.

2e Compare your notes with a partner. Explain why the information you chose to note down is relevant to assignment title 2.

3 Understanding feasibility/recommendation reports

You may find it helpful to review Unit 2 Part E on the structure of feasibility/recommendation reports before continuing with this section.

The typical aims of feasibility/recommendation reports are:

* to decide if a plan of action is possible (feasible)
* to compare two or more options and make a recommendation about which one is best.

In both types of report, the writer evaluates one or more things, summarizes their conclusions, and then makes a recommendation based on these conclusions. However, the parts of the report differ slightly.

Feasibility report	Recommendation report
• Introduction	• Introduction
• Background	• Background
• Presentation of proposed plan	• Presentation of two or more options
• Requirements that the proposed plan must satisfy	• Requirements that either option must satisfy
• Evaluation of how well the plan satisfies the requirements	• Comparison of all options to see how well they meet the requirements
• Conclusions	• Conclusions
• Recommendation about whether to proceed with the plan or not	• Recommendation of a particular option
• References	• References

In this section of the unit task, you will read more information related to your chosen assignment title, to help you prepare to do research in the following stage of the unit task.

Assignment 1
Assess the feasibility of different techniques for providing fresh water to arid regions of the world. Write a report about arid regions in general, or concentrate on the needs of a specific area.

a   This text gives an overview of different approaches to water supply. First, skim read it to identify what the different approaches to water supply are.

Water management: traditional and alternative approaches

Williamson, F. (2010). Water management: traditional and alternative approaches. *International Resource Management, 15*(2), 227–231.

Twentieth-century water resources planning tended to be based on the belief that growing population and continued economic growth would demand ever-increasing volumes of water. As a result, large-scale water supply infrastructure such as dams, reservoirs, massive water transfer projects and large-scale groundwater pumping tended to be seen as the only viable solution to the problem of water supply. In recent years the development of large-scale infrastructural projects has, to an extent, fallen out of favour, and there has been a shift towards smaller-scale solutions which focus less on supplying more water than on efficient management of existing water supplies (Gleick, 2000). This article summarizes some of the large-scale water supply projects and compares them with newer approaches to water management.

Large-scale water infrastructure
Throughout the second half of the twentieth century, demands on the world's water supplies increased massively. This was the result of a combination of factors: population increase, economic growth, and unchallenged assumptions about our right to use water in the way that suited us (World Water Assessment Programme, 2009). Global water withdrawals rose from an estimated 580 km^3 in the year 1900 to 3,700 km^3 by the turn of the 21st century (Gleick, 2000, p.129). As Gleick points out, this actual rise in water demand was assumed to be a permanent state, especially given the importance of continued economic growth in models of human development. Consequently, predictions of water use in the future all indicated constantly increasing demands for water supplies, in massive quantities. Against a background of massive future water demand, the answer seemed to be to invest in massive water infrastructure: dams; water transfers (diverted rivers or the construction of new canals); large reservoirs; or even, in regions without sufficient surface water, the pumping of deep groundwater reserves.

It is probably fair to say that the era of large-scale water supply projects is coming to an end as a result of growing awareness of the economic, environmental and social costs of such ambitious plans. Nevertheless, investment in large-scale water infrastructure has brought significant benefits, and there is probably a place for it still, in certain circumstances. Large dams helped boost economic development through the supply of hydroelectric power, which currently accounts for about 20% of all power generation (World Water Assessment Programme, 2009, p.118), while the creation of reliable supplies of water also raised food production levels in many areas of the world. Perhaps most importantly, millions of people around the world now have access to sanitation and clean drinking water as a direct consequence of improvements in water supply.

Despite the undeniable benefits that have resulted from increased supply, large-scale water projects are now falling out of favour as awareness of their drawbacks grows. One of the most significant issues, given the size of many of these projects, is cost: engineering mega-projects on the scale of the Hoover or Aswan High Dams are exceptionally expensive. To the original cost for materials and construction must be added secondary costs such as financial compensation for residents forced to move from land where projects are being completed, as well as running and maintenance costs for the lifespan of the structure. The economic costs of many such projects eventually outweigh their direct financial returns, and require substantial government subsidies. In an era of straitened budgets, such expenses are often seen as a distinct drawback to projects of this sort.

There are other costs besides the financial ones. For all that large-scale water supplies have helped to improve sanitation and access to clean drinking water on the one hand, it is also widely recognized that they can increase the incidence of waterborne diseases when large bodies of water are introduced. This is a problem in tropical regions in particular. A secondary public health problem associated with structures is the knock-on effect of dislocating large numbers of people to make way for the building projects. People moved from land that they have relied on for generations are often unprepared for the change in their living circumstances, and may end up in squalid conditions in poorly planned or constructed accommodation far from their homes. Besides immediate health risks, the psychological disturbance of being moved, perhaps into a situation where there is no work, can result in a higher incidence of psychological problems.

These projects also bring environmental costs: large water engineering projects almost inevitably require huge changes to the landscapes in which they are built, with consequent destruction of habitats for local wildlife. This can feed back into problems for local people who rely on the wildlife for their livelihoods. A poignant example of this is the fate of the Aral Sea in Central Asia: as a result of massive water withdrawals for irrigation projects from the rivers feeding the Aral Sea, the water level in the sea began dropping rapidly in the 1960s. By the year 2007 the sea had almost vanished, a mere 10% of its size half a century before. What little water was left had become highly contaminated with salt and industrial pollutants. The once vibrant fishing economy in the area around the Aral Sea collapsed completely (Micklin, 2007).

Ultimately, the greatest problem with large-scale water projects is that, for all their size, they fail to fully satisfy the water needs of the people living in the regions or nations where they are built (Gleick, 2000). In 2006, approximately 2.5 billion people were unserved with proper sanitation, and a further 800 million were without reliable drinking water supplies (WHO/UNICEF, 2010, pp.45–46). Water scarcity is in fact growing worse, with impacts on food productivity, health, and conflict in many areas of the world.

Sustainable approaches to water supply

Recent decades have seen a change in values and a shift away from large-scale projects. Growing awareness of the environmental, social and financial consequences of large-scale projects (and, crucially, the interrelationship between these issues) has led to a refocusing of attention on smaller-scale or alternative solutions which have fewer negative impacts. Though there may still be a case for large-scale projects to boost economic development or minimal water supply in some areas of the world, the trend in developed nations is in fact in the opposite direction. Gleick notes that 500 dams in the USA have been removed (2000, p.130). However, there is still a long way to go: according to the World Commission on Dams, there were over 45,000 large dams around the world in 1999 (WCD, 2001, cited in Stanley & Doyle, 2003, p.15). There is a growing sense that large-scale projects can neither meet immediate human needs, nor meet future water needs in a sustainable manner. The smaller-scale, more sustainable approaches to water supply could be grouped into two categories: new supply approaches, and a new approach to the way existing water use is managed.

New approaches to supply include conventional small-scale solutions, often based on ancient water management techniques, as well as finding innovative, non-conventional water sources. Micro-dams are a good example of conventional small-scale solutions: instead of building one massive dam, with all of its associated drawbacks, a series of smaller micro-dams is able to guarantee reliable water supplies in a way which is both cost effective and does not damage the existing environment. Micro-dams also usefully serve local areas with hydroelectricity (Clarke, 1991, p.163). Another conventional approach is so-called rainwater harvesting – essentially the collection of rainwater in tanks or small-scale reservoirs, which can be filtered for direct human consumption. This maximizes the amount of freshwater use in a

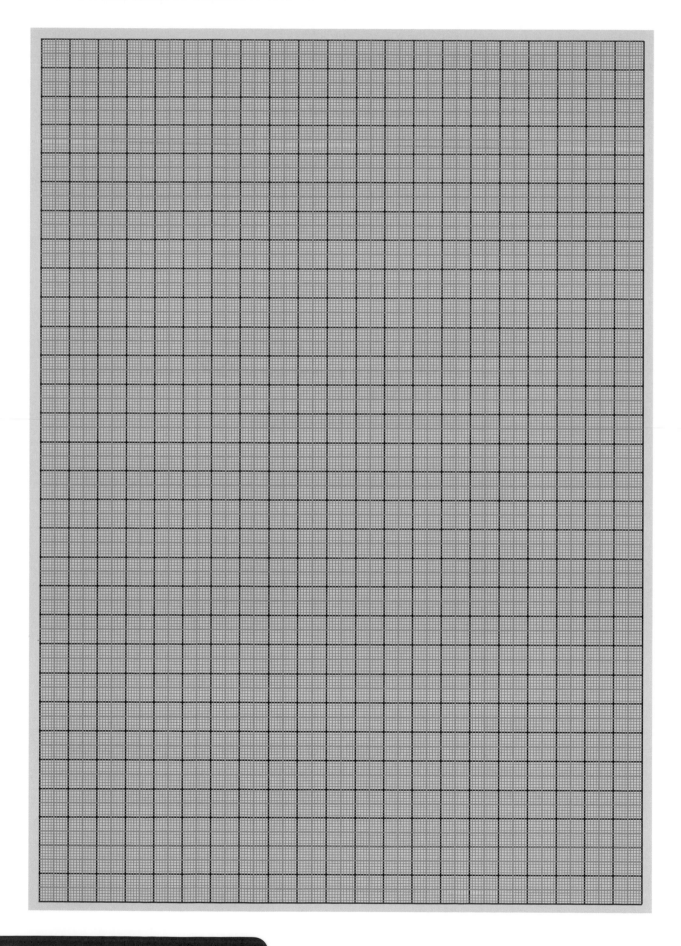

Part 2: Changing the salinity of the medium

In this experiment, you are going to change the salinity of the medium by adding salt to the water. You will try three different concentrations of salt.

Equipment

1   3 × 1-litre bottles

2   Salt

3   Teaspoon

Before you begin the experiment, fill each of the three bottles with 1 litre of ordinary tap water.

Dissolve 3 heaped teaspoonfuls of salt into the first bottle.

Dissolve 6 heaped teaspoonfuls into the second bottle.

Dissolve 9 heaped teaspoonfuls into the third bottle.

Experimental Procedure

1   Set up the equipment as before.

2   Prepare a second results table in your logbook. Think about how many rows and columns you will need to record the data for the different concentrations of salt.

3   Fill the beaker with water from the first bottle.

4   Repeat the experimental procedure from Part 1.

5   Empty the beaker, and refill it with water from the second bottle.

6   Repeat the experimental procedure from Part 1.

7   Empty the beaker, and refill it with water from the third bottle.

8   Repeat the experimental procedure from Part 1.

Go to the checklist on p.241. Look again at the tips relating to Unit 2 Part A and tick (✓) those you have used in your studies. Read the tips relating to Unit 2 Part B.

Investigating

By the end of Part C you will be able to:

- understand the research process
- understand primary and secondary research
- analyze the process of choosing a research question
- write research proposals.

1 Understanding the research process

1a The process of researching a topic can be divided into three basic stages. Put the stages (a–c) in the correct order.

> **a** Decide if the data answers the question or proves the hypothesis
>
> **b** Create a research question or hypothesis
>
> **c** Research to gather data

> Most research questions cannot be answered reliably without gathering data. For example, in order to answer the question 'What effect does income level have on access to drinking water in developing countries?', the following data would need to be gathered:
>
> **1** The average amounts of water used by people of different income levels in a developing country (or countries).
>
> **2** The methods by which people access their drinking water (e.g. private tap, community well, etc.).

1b Work in pairs. Look at these questions and hypotheses. What kind of data or information would you need to collect in order to answer the questions, or attempt to prove the hypotheses?

1 How feasible is a proposed new dam?

2 How can the efficiency of paper production be improved so that less water is used in the process?

3 What are the economic impacts of flood and drought in Ethiopia?

4 How can the quality of drinking water in a municipal water supply be improved?

5 Children's education in the poorest developing countries is affected by the amount of time that they spend travelling to collect water each day.

6 Household water use can be halved by increasing taxes on water.

7 Water scarcity affects economic growth.

8 Building large reservoirs can trigger earthquakes.

2 Understanding primary and secondary research

> In order to get information that will help you to answer your research question, you must gather data. Methods for researching information tend to fall into two types.
>
> **1 Primary research**
> This uses information which the researcher gathers by themselves, through direct observation, testing or experiment. Primary research is often used where no data exists in other sources, or if the researcher wants to check earlier data or data collection methods. Primary research is most common in postgraduate courses of all types, though undergraduates studying science will also perform a type of primary research in laboratory experiments.
>
> **2 Secondary research**
> This uses information gathered by other people in earlier studies. This tends to be common for undergraduate students in business, arts and humanities courses. However, postgraduate students and undergraduates studying science will still need to be able to do background research on other people's work as a supplement to their own primary research.

2a Work in pairs. Look at the different sources of information below. Decide which are primary and which secondary.

a experiment	e encyclopaedia	i field test	m journal article
b website	f newspaper	j magazine	n public records
c questionnaire	g report	k book	o direct observation
d face-to-face interview	h dictionary	l research by letter or email	

Primary source	Secondary source

2b Discuss which types of research, and information sources, are most common in your chosen field.

3 Analyzing the process of choosing a research question

> Choosing a question to research can be difficult, because you may not have a very clear idea of what exactly you want to research when you begin.

3a Work in pairs. Put these steps in the process of choosing a research question in the correct order.

a List all the possible questions that you want to answer about the topic	
b Select a topic that interests you	1
c Focus on the most important question	
d Proofread and revise the question	
e Think about whether the question can be researched or not	
f Define all key words and variables	
g Consider whether the question is too broad or too narrow	

3b Compare your ideas with another pair of students – do you have the same ideas about the process?

> Some research questions are interesting, and perhaps worth studying, but it is unwise to choose them if practical problems like cost or the time available make it impossible to research them properly. It is important to be realistic about whether a question can be studied, even if it is interesting in itself. Factors which might make it difficult to research a particular question can include:
> - difficulty finding the resources that you need to complete the research
> - difficulty carrying out a piece of research that you do not have the experience or ability to complete
> - problems with finding and measuring suitable data.

3c Work in pairs. Read through the scenarios 1–3 then use the checklist on p.95 to help you decide if each person's research question is practical.

1 Max is a postgraduate student planning to do some research about water desalination. He has always been interested in water resource issues. His first degree was in economics, and he wrote a very successful paper about economics and water supplies. Recently he has been reading about nuclear-powered desalination technology and thinks it could be an interesting topic. He has three months to complete his research project.

Research question: 'To what extent is a proposed nuclear desalination plant technically feasible?'

2 Jo is a second-year undergraduate student. She has been asked to complete a short piece of research about the water supplies in a local city, where the municipal water is supplied by a private company. Recently there was a water shortage in the city, and people complained that it was because the company had not been investing enough money in the water system. She has decided to research the following question:

'Was lack of investment the reason for the recent water shortage?'

Jo has searched online for financial information about the water company but found nothing. She will have to contact the company directly to request the financial data from them.

3 Mario is an overseas student completing a university foundation course in the UK. He enjoys living in the UK, but has met few local people, and spends most of his time with fellow international students. He needs to complete a short piece of research for one of his courses. He has six weeks to complete the research and has chosen to investigate British people's opinions of different brands of bottled water. His research question is: 'What factors do British people consider when choosing what bottled water to buy?'

He is planning to interview 150 people.

Checklist

Resource factors

a How much time do you have available? How long will the study take?

b How much money will it cost to do the study? Do you have enough money to cover the costs?

c What facilities or equipment will you need to complete the study?

d Will you need the help of any other people to conduct the study?

Ability factors

e Do you have the relevant experience to carry out this study successfully?

f Do you have the skills necessary to carry out the study successfully?

g Do you have the personal qualities necessary?

Factors concerning the type of data you want to gather

h Is it possible to actually measure the variables that you want to study?

i Is it possible to find suitable test subjects / participants?

j Are there any ethical implications in gathering this type of data?

Introduction

The introduction to a research proposal is similar to introductions for other types of academic text. However, there are some features which are specific to this type of introduction.

Typical features of an introduction to a research proposal can include:

1 introductory sentence
2 brief, general background information to give context
3 statement of a problem or issue that you want to investigate
4 statement of what you aim to achieve by doing the project
5 statement of the benefits of the research.

4b Look at the example introductions (1 and 2), and number any of the features above that you find.

1

It is widely recognized that sanitation and a clean supply of drinking water may greatly improve the health of residents of slum and shanty areas. A great many studies have conclusively linked improvements in water supply with declines in waterborne diseases and mortality, and general improvements in health overall. The UN's Millennium Development Goals identify provision of clean water, or improvements of supplies to a basic minimum, as priorities (UN, 2009), though at current rates of improvement over 2.5 billion people around the world will still be without sanitation by 2015 (WHO, 2008), far short of the Millennium Goal targets. This will have direct consequences for the health of residents in deprived areas. An aspect of the sanitation problem which has been less thoroughly investigated is the way that lack of access to clean water and sanitation can increase poverty itself, thus trapping poorer residents of low-income developing countries in a permanent state of poverty, poor water access and ill health. The aim of this project is to explore the water–poverty–health relationship by focusing on the way that lack of access to clean water can exacerbate the problems of poverty. It is hoped that the current study will help to increase understanding of the complex dynamics of poverty which frequently make water development goals difficult to reach.

2

Life for those who are not served with convenient water supplies poses many hardships. For many in remote communities, one of those hardships is the burden of making daily trips to wells or other water sources in order to collect water for household use. According to the seminal study of water use in East Africa by White et al. (1972), up to four hours a day could be spent by villagers collecting for their households. This burden falls particularly heavily on women and young children, who are often charged with the water-carrying task. Time spent by children carrying water frequently means a loss of time spent at school (WHO, 2005, p.14), with consequent effects on educational opportunities, and ultimately on the ability of poor families to lift themselves out of poverty through education.

Following on from studies such as that conducted by White et al. (ibid), and more recent investigations of the water-time burden in Africa (for instance Thompson et al., 2000), the aim of this study is to investigate the time spent carrying water by school-age children in a rural village in Cambodia. The data gathered in the study will be used to identify the effects that this daily activity has on the children's educational attainment. This research aims to provide further evidence for the argument that reliable water supplies are essential not just for health, but also to provide poor communities with the hope of escape from the poverty trap.

Literature review

The literature review in a research proposal is normally shorter than the literature review which would appear in a final report. A research proposal literature review should give a brief overview of the key research which has been done on the topic in order to help a non-expert reader understand the background to your study. (Literature reviews are covered in more detail in Unit 1 Part E3.)

Method

4c Work in pairs. Read the two method sections from research proposals. Make a list of the information that they typically include.

1 Method

1 Conduct a literature review of existing studies about the time children spend drawing water and its effects on time available for study.

2 The general findings from the literature review will be tested against case studies of a village in a water-stressed district where collecting water from a nearby well is the work of women and children.

3 The village's children will be observed for a period of six weeks and will participate in the study by logging the number of hours per day spent either on studying or on gathering water.

4 A smaller number of the children (approximately ten) will be interviewed about their affective response to drawing water (e.g. tiredness, distraction from study), to ascertain whether they make a conscious link between time spent drawing water and time lost to study. In order to avoid suggesting answers to the children, the interviews will not be formal or structured.

5 Teachers in the local school will participate in formal interviews to ascertain their views about the number of hours that children should be studying.

6 Time–activity results for the six weeks will be collated and analyzed using statistical software such as SPSS.

7 The results of the time–activity study will be compared against the guidelines for time spent in school given in the government's Education 2020 document.

2.1 Method

The study will use secondary research of statistical data analyzing water, poverty and associated health outcomes, as well as primary research consisting of in-depth interviews with residents about their health records.

2.2 Sample

- Water availability statistics for two neighbourhoods (one high income and one low income) covering the period 1975–2008.

- Health records (where available). These will be accessed by request from the national health register.

- Water quality survey documents accessed from local government and water company archives, as well as results of independent testing carried out by non-governmental organizations (NGOs).

- Adult individuals in 25 households in each neighbourhood.

2.3 Procedure

In the secondary stage of the research, health and water availability statistics for the two districts will be compared, attempting to find links between varying water availability and increases in episodes of ill health. Water quality data will be matched against periods when incidences of ill health increased.

In the primary stage of the research, in-depth semi-structured interviews will be carried out with occupants of 25 households in each neighbourhood, attempting to uncover details about health episodes which may not be available in public records, as well as the occupants' perceptions of the impact that their water supplies have on their health.

2.4 Limitations

Health records may not be available due to confidentiality regulations, or may only be partially complete for the period being investigated. Interviews with local residents will be used in an attempt to fill in the gaps in official health records where these exist. However, there is a risk that this will introduce a subjective element into the final results that may undermine the validity of the study.

4d Work with another pair of students. Compare your ideas about the typical contents of a methods section.

Expected results

Not all proposals include a full expected results section; however, proposals do tend to include at least a paragraph which outlines what the author is expecting to discover. This section normally includes these features:

- An indication of what results are expected
- An explanation of why these results are expected
- The possible outcomes of or benefits from the research.

At this stage of your research, you cannot be sure what you will discover, so you must express your expected results in a way which acknowledges the possibility that things may turn out differently from what you expected. It is more common to do this using impersonal language.

Useful expressions for expected results	Phrases to avoid
It is expected that …	I expect that…
It is believed that …	This research will prove that …
It is my belief that …	This research will show that …
The authors predict that …	It will be shown that …
It is likely that …	This research will show that …
Possible outcomes of the research	I will show…
include …	I will prove…
This project will identify …	
This project is expected to demonstrate	
that …	

4e Look at the example of an expected results section below. The researcher has written it in a way which does not acknowledge the possibility of different outcomes. Read through the passage and underline any expressions which you think need to be changed.

Expected results and outcomes

Given the amount of existing literature on this topic which already draws strong links between water scarcity and poverty, this project will prove that water scarcity leads both directly and indirectly to ill health. This research will show that more investment is needed to improve the quantity, reliability and quality of existing water supplies in developing nations. The research will benefit policy planners at government level, and lead to a better understanding of the relation of water and health.

4f Work in pairs. Compare your answers, then think of alternative ways to phrase this section.

Timeline

4g Look at the typical stages of a research project below. Work in pairs. Put them in the order that you think it most likely that they would be completed.

Stage	Typical order of completion
Fieldwork / data gathering	
Do preliminary reading and write proposal	1
Literature review	
Write first draft	
Analyze results	
Redrafting and completion of final report	

4h Read the scenario below and decide if the student's timeline is realistic. Explain your reasons to a partner.

Carla is writing a 5,000-word research report as part of an undergraduate course in resource management. She has decided to investigate the differences between water use in wealthy compared to poor households in a water-stressed area. She plans to interview people in 30 low-income households and 30 high-income households. She has twelve weeks to complete the research.

Carla's timeline:

Phase	Time required	Completion date
Complete proposal	3 weeks	8 October
Gather literature	2 weeks	22 October
Complete literature review	1 week	29 October
Recruit respondents	3 days	3 November
Conduct fieldwork	2 days	5 November
Complete analysis of results	3 weeks	26 November
Complete first draft	1 week	3 December
Complete final draft	1 week	10 December

Bibliography

The bibliography does not need to contain all the references that you will use in the final report, as this is just a proposal for what you will do, and at this stage you may not have read or even found all the literature that you will eventually use; it is likely that your bibliography will continue to grow as you are doing your research.

4i Work in pairs. Discuss which of these references you think should be included in a research proposal bibliography. Tick (✓) anything which you should include.

Type of source	Include?
References for texts by key thinkers	
References for the texts which you know you will definitely use in the final report	
References to useful texts which you have not read yet but are planning to use	
References only for texts which you have read thoroughly	
References to texts which give general background information on the topic	

4j Read the research proposal below and decide whether it is effective.

Water use differences

1 Introduction

Daily water needs are approximately 50 litres per person per day (Gleick, 1999). Average yearly water withdrawals per person in a given country are frequently published by organizations such as the UN and WHO. However, these average figures may obscure the fact that water demand may vary between different socioeconomic groups within a country (Meinzen-Dick & Appasamy, 2002, p.29). Furthermore, the uses to which water is put may also vary (McDonald and Ruiters, 2005). The aim of the proposed research is to discover whether households at different socioeconomic levels in Nairobi differ in their patterns of water use, and the daily quantity of water that they use, depending on their wealth.

2 Research questions

Three research questions will be addressed in this study:

1 What differences exist in per capita water withdrawals among households of different socioeconomic level?

2 What differences exist in the ways water is used in these households?

3 What is the relationship between accessibility and the quantity of water used?

3 Literature review

My literature review will be based on studies of water use among different socioeconomic groups, particularly McDonald and Ruiters (2005), and the famous study by White et al. (1972), because both of these books deal with water use in Africa.

4 Method

Two types of data will be gathered for the study: (1) numerical data of water volumes used; (2) residents' explanations of their water allocation decisions.

As the main focus of the study is on measurements of water in use, a quantitative approach has been adopted for the data collection. This will allow for easier collection of data, as well as the comparison between the findings in different households.

4.1 Sample

30 households will be chosen in different districts of the city. The districts will be divided into low, middle and high income based on the results of the latest population census figures available. Ten households will be chosen in each district.

4.2 Procedure

Questionnaires will be distributed to each household. The respondents must complete the questionnaire explaining how many litres of water they use in total each day, and how many litres of water they use for different purposes such as drinking, cooking and hygiene.

5 Expected results

Based on the findings from earlier studies, it is expected that this research will prove that amount of water use varies with economic level. Moreover, this research will show that people in poorer households differ from those in richer households in the ways they use water.

6 Timeline

Phase	Time required	Completion date
Complete proposal	2 weeks	17 February
Gather literature	1 week	24 February
Complete literature review	3 weeks	16 March
Gather data	3 weeks	6 April
Complete final draft	2 weeks	20 April

7 References

Gleick, P. (1999). The human right to water. *Water Policy*, *1*(5), 487–503.

McDonald, D.A., & Ruiters, G. (Eds.) (2005). *The Age of Commodity: Water Privatization in Southern Africa*. London: Earthscan.

Meinzen-Dick, R., & Appasamy, P.P. (2002). Urbanization and intersectoral competition for water. In *Finding the source: The linkages between population and water. Woodrow Wilson International Centre for Scholars. Environmental Change and Security Project*, pp.27–51. Washington: Woodrow Wilson International Centre for Scholars.

White, G.F., Bradley, D.J., & White, A.U. (1972). *Drawers of Water: domestic water use in East Africa*. Chicago: University of Chicago Press.

4k Work in small groups. Compare and explain your evaluations of the report.

> **UNIT TASK** **Water research project**

In this section of the Unit Task, you will complete some research relating to the assignment that you have chosen. Read the detailed instructions below for your assignment title.

Assignment 1

Assess the feasibility of different techniques for providing fresh water to arid regions of the world. Write a report about arid regions in general, or concentrate on the needs of a specific area.

In this section of the unit task you will search for sources of information which will help you to compare the feasibility of different water sources.

a   Work in small groups to brainstorm possible search terms that you can use to find sources online or in your university library. Make a note of your ideas.

Search terms

b   Search for possible sources individually. Skim read any sources that you find to decide if they could be useful.

c   Hold a meeting with the other members of your group to introduce the sources you have found to them.

d   Work in groups. Prepare a reference list of the sources that you think are most useful. The reference list should be properly formatted for Harvard style references. (You may find it useful to review Unit 1 Part C before doing this.)

e   Share the reference list with other groups in your class.

Assignment 2

Conduct an experiment to measure the refractive index of water.

In this section of the unit task you will carry out the laboratory experiment to measure the refractive index of water.

a   Before you begin, review the information about keeping a logbook in Unit 1 Part C4.

b   Read through the lab instructions again to ensure that you understand them.

c   Prepare pages to record your observations and results in a separate logbook. Make a note of any relevant theoretical background in the logbook before starting the experiment.

d   While you conduct the experiment, take careful notes in your logbook.

e   After the experiment, reflect on your notes and add any other questions or comments that occur to you.

f   Consider any unexpected results that you observed. Work in pairs. Discuss the possible reasons for these results and make notes of them in the logbook.

g   Work in pairs. Design an experiment to measure the refractive index of water at different temperatures.

 Go to the checklist on p.241. Look again at the tips relating to Unit 2 Parts A–B and tick (✓) those you have used in your studies. Read the tips relating to Unit 2 Part C.

Reporting in speech

By the end of Part D you will be able to:

- participate in seminar discussions
- exchange and challenge ideas appropriately in academic discussion
- express and defend opinions
- change the direction of a discussion
- conclude a discussion.

1 Participating in seminar discussions

1a Work in small groups. Think of reasons for having group discussions and how students can benefit from them.

1b Work in pairs. You are going to discuss the question below.

You work for a company which is thinking of launching a new water drink made from recycled waste water. How feasible do you think this business plan would be?

Recycled waste water is effectively sewage which has been specially purified to make it safe. Discuss briefly your opinion of the business plan.

1c Read the introductory passage and make some notes to support your ideas in the space below.

Recycled drinking water: how realistic is it?

Nations around the world are facing increasingly severe problems of water supply. Even in those parts of the world where rainfall is plentiful, over-consumption by the human population can mean that water supplies still run short. With population growth, demand is increasing all the time. Though we have often acted in the past as though supplies of drinking water were limitless, we must, these days, be more realistic about our water use, and find more efficient and creative ways of supplying our basic needs.

One possible solution is the use of recycled waste water. This is known officially as reclaimed water: effectively it is domestic sewage which has been treated to remove impurities, and then returned to use for the community. Several projects around the world have successfully used reclaimed water in this way for industrial and irrigation purposes; relatively few attempts have been made to convince the human population to accept this as a source of drinking water, however. Though reclaimed water undergoes a very thorough treatment process which makes it entirely safe to drink (and often cleaner than municipal tap water supplies) one obvious problem is public resistance to the idea of drinking treated sewage: people simply do not trust that it is safe, or they find the thought of it literally distasteful.

One example of a reclaimed drinking water enterprise comes from Singapore, a nation which suffers constant water stress and has been forced to adopt innovative methods to meet its water demands. A product known as NEWater was developed in the late 1990s as part of a feasibility scheme to see if Singapore could improve its domestic water resource efficiency. NEWater is created from waste water which has been subjected to an intense purification process. Currently, five NEWater factories produce about 30% of Singapore's daily water needs. Though it is mainly intended for use in industry, it is perfectly safe to drink, and bottles of it were offered to the Singaporean public as part of a publicity drive to improve the public perception of this type of water source. The bottles resembled branded mineral water bottles and were 'marketed' as a fashionable new drink. Though they were not sold commercially, they have become very popular items. Most NEWater, however, is fed into the city's water supplies, where it blends with other conventional water sources and so forms a small part of the tap water in the city (about 1% of daily consumption). Nevertheless, the Singaporean public's acceptance of this water source indicates that there is a possible business market for sales of bottled water which have been reclaimed in this way.

1d Work in small groups. Discuss whether you feel that it is feasible to sell a drink made from recycled water. Use your notes to support your opinion.

1e Work in pairs to reflect on what you said. Discuss whether you did any of these things.

- Gave your opinion
- Voiced agreement with another speaker
- Challenged another speaker's ideas
- Encouraged another person to give their opinion

1f Work in pairs. Discuss how well you think you contributed to the conversation. Give yourself a score between 1 and 5 (5 = most successful).

> A group discussion is an opportunity for the whole group to share information and develop ideas together. Group discussions are most effective if every member of the group participates.

1g Work in pairs. Discuss how well you participated in a recent group discussion by giving yourself a score between 1 and 5 (5 = most successful) for each of the points in the table below.

My contribution to discussions	Your score	Partner's score
I ask questions to keep the discussion going or to clarify points which I do not understand.		
I listen carefully to what others are saying.		
I contribute fully to the discussion and give my opinions and ideas.		
I encourage other members of the group to participate.		
My body language shows that I am interested, open-minded and paying attention.		
I allow other people to express their ideas.		
I consider other people's ideas, even if at first I think I disagree with them.		

1h Work in groups. Half of the group should brainstorm possible answers to this question:

What methods could be used to raise public acceptance for a NEWater-style municipal water supply created from recycled waste water?

The other half of the group should brainstorm answers to this question:

In what ways could a NEWater-style bottled water, produced from recycled waste water, be marketed for sale in shops?

1i Work in the same groups. Half of the group should have a group discussion about their question. The other half of the group should listen and give each person participating in the discussion a score between 1 and 5. Then change so that the other half of the group discusses.

1j Work in pairs to share feedback on the group discussion. Decide on the group's and individuals' strong and weak points and think of ways that they could improve.

1k Work in the same group of eight as you did in 1h. Give the other half of the group feedback on their discussion.

2 Exchanging and challenging ideas appropriately in academic discussion

2a You are about to listen to a discussion which is going wrong because of the way that the participants are expressing themselves. Before you listen, work in small groups to predict ways that a discussion might go wrong, and make notes.

Notes
don't be nife
whad do you meen by just ~~kno~~ NO
non -refrence

2b Listen to check your predictions. Add any other problems you hear to your notes.

2.8

2c Work in small groups. Compare your answers to 2a and 2b.

2d Work in small groups. Discuss why the **bold** expressions in discussions 1–3 are not appropriate. Then think of alternatives that would help the conversation to flow more smoothly. Give your reasons to the other members of your group.

1 **Mike:** OK, so we need to think of ways that we can improve public opinions about the idea of drinking reused water. Leila, any ideas?

Leila: Well, you can give away free samples …

Sam: **That won't work**. People aren't going to drink treated sewage even if you give it away for free. **That's a complete no-brainer**.

2 **Leila:**   No, you can make it look nice and have famous people drinking it.

   Sam: **Don't be naive**. Consumers these days are wise to that kind of marketing. They'll be suspicious and it won't work. **You have to have a more intelligent strategy** which involves educating the consumer and giving them the facts – treating them like intelligent adults.

   Mike: Like what?

   Sam: You know. **Give them facts and data**, that's all.

   Leila: Yeah, but like what? What kind of facts? **You can't just say 'Give them facts'. That's meaningless**.

3 **Sam:**   And where was this study done?

   Mike: **How should I know?** Anyway, I agree with Sam, you've got to give them facts. That can be the first point.

3   Expressing and defending opinions

> Before continuing with this section, you might find it helpful to review Unit 1 Part D Section 2 – discussing data.
>
> To participate successfully in a group discussion, you should be ready to offer your own opinions. It is likely that another of your group may challenge your ideas, so you should be ready to defend them. Basing your ideas on evidence can be an effective way of doing this.

3a   You are working on a project to raise public acceptance of a bottled water product made from recycled waste water and want to answer this question: Are customers likely to accept a bottled water made from recycled waste water? Work in groups of four or five students. Complete the table below with your answer to the question and reasons.

Are customers likely to accept a bottled water made from recycled waste water?	
Your own opinion: For/against?	Reason/explanations for your opinion

3b Look at the sets of data below. Find evidence which would support your answer in 3a.

a

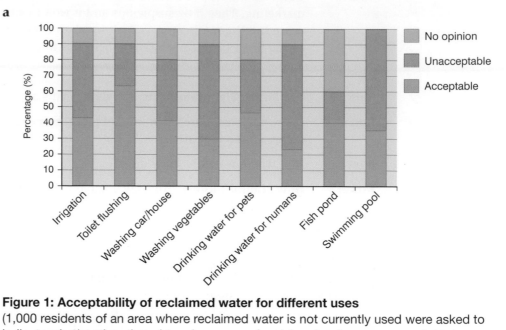

Figure 1: Acceptability of reclaimed water for different uses
(1,000 residents of an area where reclaimed water is not currently used were asked to indicate whether they thought various uses of reclaimed water were acceptable.)

b

Table 1: Self-rating of understanding of water issues

Rating	Very limited knowledge	Limited knowledge	Fair amount of knowledge	Detailed knowledge	No opinion	Total
Knowledge of water issues	38	78	16	7	11	150

(150 residents of an area where reclaimed water is used for non-potable use were asked to rate their own knowledge about their water supply. This included questions about how municipal water is treated, the chemical purity of the water, and how quality checks are conducted.)

c

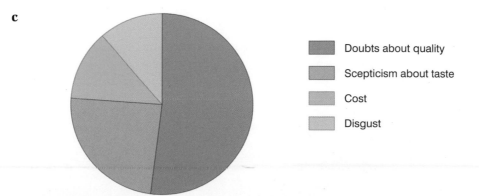

Figure 2: Primary reason for reluctance to drink reclaimed water
(Based on a sample of 100 individuals who identified themselves as reluctant to drink reclaimed water.)

d

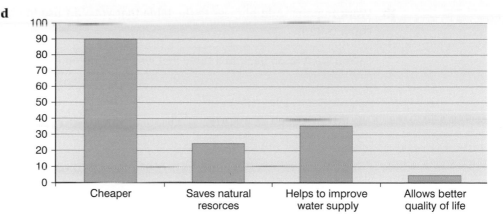

Figure 3: Benefits of using reclaimed water
(100 residents of an area where reclaimed water is used for non-potable use were asked to identify the benefits of using this type of water.)

e

Table 2: Results of a taste test*

Rating (%) \ Type	Disliked intensely	Disliked	Neutral	Liked	Liked intensely	Total
Reclaimed water	10	13	46	28	3	100%
Branded mineral water	3	14	26	46	11	100%
Municipal tap water	9	22	19	48	2	100%

* From a survey conducted with 1000 adults. The participants knew what each type of water was before they drank it.

3c Work in groups of four or five students. Discuss the question in 3a. Use evidence from the data to support your answer.

3d Work in pairs. Discuss these questions.

1 What opinions did you offer during the discussion?
2 What evidence did you use to support your opinions?
3 Were any of your ideas challenged by other members of the group?
4 How did you defend your ideas against challenges?
5 How successful were you at offering and defending your opinions?

4 Changing the direction of a discussion

4a Look at phrases 1–3 from a discussion and match them with functions a–c in the table in 4b.

1 'A separate point I'd like to discuss is public opinion.'
2 'Can we just go back to what Liz said about costs for a moment?'
3 'Why don't we consider the technical aspects in more detail?'

4b Work in pairs. Add phrases to the table that you can use to change the direction of a conversation.

a You want to go back to a topic that was considered earlier in the discussion.

b You want to move the discussion on to a different aspect of the topic.

c You want to change the topic completely.

4c You have been asked to complete a small group project with this title:

Investigate the issues that a city council would face if it tried to introduce reclaimed water (from treated sewage) for both drinking and non-drinking uses. Investigate the feasibility of such a scheme.

Work in groups of three. Choose one of the objectives cards below and brainstorm suggestions and requests you could make in a discussion.

Objective card A

Your objectives in the discussion:

1 Decide where you will get information about reclaimed water.

2 Decide how each person will contribute to the project.

Objective card B

Your objectives in the discussion:

1 You want to brainstorm the kinds of issues that the city council would need to consider.

2 You want to find out each member of the group's opinions on whether or not such a scheme is feasible.

Objective card C

Your objectives in the discussion:

1 You want to think of search terms that you could use to begin finding information online.

2 You want to brainstorm the different aspects that you would need in order to decide if the project was feasible.

4d Work in groups of three with students who have different objective cards. Have a discussion about the project in 4c. Try to achieve the objectives on your card.

5 Concluding a discussion

5a Ultimately, the goal of any academic discussion should be to share and develop ideas. Work in pairs. Discuss why it is useful to conclude a discussion with a summary of what you have spoken about.

5b Work in small groups. Think of phrases that you can use to help to bring a discussion to a conclusion. Add them to the table on page 114.

You want to suggest to the other members of the group that it's time to finish the discussion.

You want to summarize the important details of the talk.

You want to invite the other members of the group to add any extra comments.

5c Read the assignment title below. What does it ask you to do?

'You are working on a business enterprise project. Your group is planning to introduce a new branded bottled water into the retail drinks market. The plan is to make this product from reclaimed waste water, similar to Singapore's NEWater. Prepare a feasibility report by researching other projects of this sort around the world, and making a recommendation about whether this project is possible or not.'

5d Work in groups of four. Discuss these points.

1 Brainstorm likely problems for such a project.

2 Share your ideas about the feasibility of such a business.

3 Identify the kind of information you need to begin your research project, and how you will begin to find it.

4 Bring your conversation to a conclusion. Try to use some of the phrases from 5b.

➤ UNIT TASK   Water research project

In this section of the unit task, you will take part in a group discussion with your classmates relating to the assignment title that you have chosen. Read the detailed instructions below for your assignment title.

Assignment 1

In this section of the unit task you will participate in a discussion with other members of your group to share information about different water sources.

a   Work in small groups. Choose ONE of the following titles to discuss.

    1   Identify possible techniques which can be used for providing fresh water to the world's arid areas. Discuss the advantages and disadvantages of each option, and try to decide which techniques are most feasible. Use data and information from your research to support your ideas.

    2   Large-scale water management techniques have caused too much damage; small-scale sustainable techniques should be used instead. To what extent do you agree with this statement and why?

b   Produce a poster which outlines the information on the topic that you have discovered so far, and can be used to present data to support your ideas.

c   Work with another group who chose the same title. Participate in a seminar discussion which covers the points in the discussion topic instruction above.

Assignment 2

In this section of the Unit Task you will prepare a poster to present the results of your experiment.

Poster presentation instruction

a   Produce a poster which reports the background, method and results of your laboratory experiment in Part C.

b   Work in pairs. Evaluate your posters before the presentation session. Make suggestions about how the poster could be improved.

c   Prepare for the poster session by thinking of questions that you might be asked, and consider how you will answer them.

d   In small groups, present the results of your laboratory experiment to your classmates using your poster.

Go to the checklist on p.241. Look again at the tips relating to Unit 2 Parts A–C and tick (✓) those you have used in your studies. Read the tips relating to Unit 2 Part D.

Reporting in writing

By the end of Part E you will be able to:

- understand the main features of a primary research report
- understand the main features of a successful feasibility/recommendation report
- make choices about the best way to structure your reports.

1 Understanding the main features of a primary research report

Primary research reports give an account of a piece of research done by the author. For instance, this could be a report of an experiment done in a science lab (usually known as a laboratory/lab report), or it could be an account of a piece of fieldwork. The exact content, structure and length of a report will vary depending on the level of the research; an undergraduate report is likely to be considerably shorter than a research report published in an academic journal.

Lab reports tend to fall into two types, depending on the level of study.

A Measurement of a known quantity

This tends to be more common for undergraduate science students, who must perform an experiment to measure a given quantity and compare their results against published data. An analysis of the results is performed and the results are explained in the context of a particular theory. No original hypothesis is given in the lab report.

B Hypothesis test experiment

This is perhaps more common for postgraduate students and researchers. The student will develop a hypothesis and create an experiment in order to test it. The results of the experiment will be used in a discussion about whether or not they support or contradict the hypothesis.

The following section will focus on scientific lab reports as an example of primary research reports. However, the basic format, layout and guidelines for this section are generally applicable to other types of primary research report as well.

1a Work in small groups. Discuss the types of primary research which are most common in the subject which you are studying.

1b Many researchers do not write the different sections of the report in the order in which they are eventually presented. Work in pairs. Decide which order you think it would be easiest to write the sections in, and why.

Methods	Results	Introduction	Discussion	Conclusion	Abstract
	Title		References		

A note on the language of lab reports

The lab report explains what you have done in your own research, and also discusses the general relevance and implications of your findings. As a result, different sections of the report tend to use different verb tenses.

Normally, the abstract, methods and results sections are written using past tenses, while the discussion is written using present tenses. The introduction and conclusion are normally written in a combination of past and present tenses.

Passive voice versus active voice

There is some debate about whether the active voice or passive voice should be used for the methods section. Different academic fields and levels of study tend to have different conventions about which voice to use (for instance, it is customary for published scientific journal articles to be written in the passive voice).

Example

Active   I sealed the valve to prevent water flow.

Passive   The valve was sealed to prevent water flow.

It is a good idea to check with your course tutor to find out which style is preferred in your subject field.

2   Primary research reports – the introduction

The introduction in a research report is similar to introductions in other types of academic writing.

2a   Work in pairs. Discuss and tick (✓) which of the features below would be appropriate for an introduction to a primary research report.

A research report introduction might include:	✓
1 A general introduction to the topic	
2 A description of background information or theory relevant to the study	
3 A description of aspects of the study already investigated by other researchers	
4 A consideration of the strengths and weaknesses of these other studies	
5 A statement that an area of the subject needs more investigation	
6 A statement of the objective of your study	
7 An explanation of why you chose the method that you used for your study	
8 A justification of the value of the study	
9 An explanation that the experiment was successful	
10 A brief summary of the methods used	
11 A hypothesis that you will test in the research	
12 A brief discussion of the results of the experiment	
13 An explanation of special equipment used in the experiment	

5 Separate subsections for 'Materials' and 'Methods'	
6 A list of instructions for how to carry out the experiment	
7 Detailed explanations of all the equipment you used	
8 Detailed explanations of any non-standard equipment or procedures that you used	
9 The precision of any measuring equipment you used	
10 A discussion of how you could improve the method in future	
11 Citations for standard procedures created by other people	

3c Work in pairs and discuss your answers to 3b.

3d The information in the example methods section below is probably too specific – it gives details which are unnecessary. Rewrite this section so that it contains only necessary information.

Materials and methods

Materials

1 Header tank to supply water under pressure
2 Control valve to control the water supply
3 Two metal pipes of different length and diameter (0.6m long by 9.9mm diameter and 2.58m by 3.85mm)
4 Three tall, transparent plastic tanks which rise from different parts of the pipe
5 Small, thin pieces of Blu-Tack to measure the level of the water
6 Large glass beaker for collecting run-off water
7 Large glass measuring cylinder to measure the water which runs off
8 Tape measure to measure the height of the water
9 Stopwatch to time the flow rate for one minute

Method

1 The length of the two pipe sections was measured and recorded in the logbook.
2 The diameter of the pipe sections was measured and recorded in the logbook.
3 Small, thin pieces of Blu-Tack were stuck onto each vertical tube to show the level of the water when the flow rate was zero.
4 The header tank was filled with water and the control valve was opened to allow water to flow.
5 The control valve was adjusted so that there was a gentle flow of water into the final tank. The water levels in the vertical tubes were observed until they settled.
6 Water from the overflow was collected in a large beaker for precisely one minute timed on a stopwatch by my partner William.
7 Spilled water was mopped up with a cloth.
8 The water was poured into a large measuring cylinder and the flow rate was recorded in cm³ in the results table in the logbook.

9 The measurement was repeated three times by my partner and me to ensure a reliable and consistent flow rate.

10 A tape measure was used by myself to measure the height of the water above the Blu-Tack marks for zero flow rate.

11 The control valve was adjusted to change the flow rate, and the measurements were repeated in the same way to obtain data for five different flow rates.

3e Work in pairs. Compare your answers to 3d. Decide on the best version of the methods section.

> The methods section should not just be a set of instructions. Instead, it should explain what you have done in your own research. It should give enough information for two purposes: so that you can repeat your own study again in future if need be, and so that another researcher in the future can read (or copy) what you did to evaluate the scientific validity of your research.
>
> The materials and methods section can be written in two ways: as a list or as a narrative explanation. If the section is written as a list, it should still be written using past tenses. A common mistake is to copy the list of instructions from a lab manual, which are normally written in the present simple tense. You should not copy these generalized instructions, but instead explain what you did (as this may differ from the original instructions).

3f The example methods section given in 3d above is in list style. Compare this with a narrative style below. Work in pairs. Discuss which style you prefer.

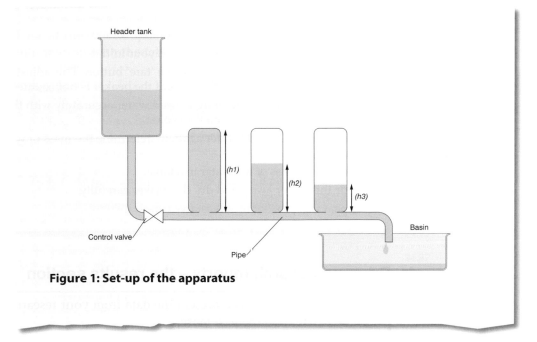

Figure 1: Set-up of the apparatus

Ease of use/instruction

The system should not be so complicated that users are unable to operate it effectively. Furthermore, it is intended that the knowledge of how to use the system can be taught to other households, or explained to younger family members. It should therefore be of a level of difficulty which makes this process as simple as possible. Any system should be able to be explained verbally, and not rely on complicated written technical instructions.

Availability of parts

This relates partly to cost, but also to supply in regions which are, by definition, remote. The system should, to the largest extent possible, use parts which are cheaply available and abundant locally.

Actual water quality

The quality of the water produced by the system should meet or exceed minimum standards for human consumption.

Perceived water quality (taste)

Even if the water can be tested to demonstrate that it is chemically safe, the system will not be adopted if the consumers who will eventually drink it dislike the taste. Therefore the system needs to produce water which residents/consumers judge to be fit for their own consumption based on their impressions of its taste.

Quantity of water delivered

Humans require about five litres of water per capita per day for drinking and food preparation. The system should therefore be able to reliably produce a suitable quantity of water.

The requirements could be presented in a separate section, or may appear in the introduction or background, depending on the length of the report.

9a It is common to express requirements using unambiguous modal verbs such as *must*. Read example b and underline any similar expressions. Which expressions are used most commonly?

9b Look at the reports in **Appendices 4** and **5** again. Where are the requirements explained?

10 Feasibility/recommendation reports – comparison/evaluation of options

This section of the report describes key features of the option being considered. It explains particular advantages or disadvantages in enough detail so that the person reading the report has all the information they need to make a sensible decision.

When structuring a recommendation report containing two or more alternatives, the comparisons may be structured in different ways:

1 Separate sections for each option, considering each option's features in turn

2 Separate sections for each feature, comparing each of the options on that point

10a Look at the two possible comparison sections below, for a report about different drinking water supplies in an office. How have the different aspects of each option been dealt with?

Example A

Comparison

1 Existing tap water supply

The existing tap water supply is connected to the municipal water mains. Taps dispensing potable water are located in the staff kitchen and toilets: the existing tap water therefore provides a reliable and constant supply of water to all members of staff, which is convenient to access. In terms of cost, this is probably one of the cheaper options, as the building is non-metered and pays a standard rate of £638 per year at the time of writing. This does not vary with the amount of water used. While many staff feel that this is an acceptable supply of water, a significant number of staff members complain that the taste of the water from the taps is unpleasant. In an unofficial survey many members of staff complained that they did not trust the quality of the water direct from the taps, even if the taste was acceptable.

2 Retail vending machine

A number of companies offer leased and serviced retail beverage vending machines. One significant benefit of this option is that it would provide other cold soft drinks besides water, and thus cater for a range of tastes. Costs for the rental of vending machines vary considerably depending on size and rental or leasing agreements. However, an average price of around £500 a year (to the company) seems possible. The acceptability of such a system to the staff members is uncertain, as they would be required to pay for their drinks. Nevertheless, the quality of the product vended would be guaranteed. The vending machine would be serviced and restocked on a weekly basis.

3 Serviced water cooler

Serviced water coolers are a popular option in many offices and are therefore likely to be easily accepted by staff. They provide fresh, clean water of a guaranteed quality and taste, at no cost to staff members. Costs for the company would depend on the type of machine, servicing contract, and standard orders for bottle deliveries. However, after the initial outlay for the machine (approximately £170), we estimate that the company's drinking water needs could be met for about £830 per year. This is considerably more than the other two options. Supply would be guaranteed as part of the contract with the supplier, and therefore we could be sure of a reliable supply.

Example B

Comparison

• Cost

The serviced water cooler is likely to be the most expensive of the three options from the company's point of view: an initial outlay of approximately £170 would be required for the machine, followed by a monthly contract from deliveries of bottles of water. Based on staff numbers and estimated consumption, we calculate that this would cost a further £830 per year. However, staff would not have to pay any costs for this service. A cheaper option from the company's point of view is to lease a vending machine which would sell cold beverages to staff. Costs for these vary but a machine costing approximately £500 per year seems reasonable. Staff would, of course, have to pay for each drink that they bought. The cheapest option from the company's point of view is to use only the municipal water dispensed through the taps. This would not be considered an 'extra' cost by the company, as it is already factored into running costs for the premises (currently £638 per year). There would be no cost to staff.

Assignment 2

In this section of the unit task you will use the data you recorded in your logbook to write up a full primary research / lab report for the experiment.

Your tutor will tell you how long the report should be.

a Before you begin, consider these points:

1 Will you use active or passive voice to write your report?

2 Will you present the materials and methods in the same section or separate sections?

3 Will you use a list style or narrative style to present your methods?

4 What will you include in your discussion section?

b Use the space below to plan your report.

Title	
Key information for introduction	

Section titles	Key information
1	
2	
3	
4	
5	
6	
7	

If you incorporate other writers' work into your report, use quotation, paraphrasing and summary to do this appropriately. You should give proper citations and references (following the Harvard format that you have learned in this book) for any ideas or information you use from other sources.

Go to the checklist on p.241. Look again at the tips relating to Unit 2 Parts A–D and tick (✓) those you have used in your studies. Read the tips relating to Unit 2 Part E.

Unit 3   Progress

Unit overview

Part	This part will help you to ...	By improving your ability to ...
A	**Follow sequences of ideas**	• follow descriptions of processes and sequences • follow an account of the development of ideas over time • follow a description of a manufacturing process • follow a description of a lab procedure.
B	**Read critically**	• follow written processes • interpret process diagrams and flow charts • evaluate processes • critically analyze reported statistics.
C	**Develop and express your own position on a topic**	• draw conclusions from data • deal with sources of uncertainty • avoid absolute terms • protect your position through citation • use cautious language for your own claims.
D	**Explain events and their implications**	• explain the possible implications of events • give an oral progress report.
E	**Compare literature on a topic**	• explain, compare and interpret sources • synthesize sources and viewpoints • write a progress report.

Understanding spoken information

By the end of Part A you will be able to:

- follow descriptions of processes and sequences
- follow an account of the development of ideas over time
- follow a description of a manufacturing process
- follow a description of a lab procedure.

1 Following descriptions of processes and sequences

> The ability to follow a description of a process or procedure is important for most academic subjects. This could, for instance, be a description of the process by which an item of equipment operates, or the sequence of steps for a piece of research. The development of ideas or theories on a particular topic may also be explained as a process of development.

1a Listen to excerpts from the descriptions of three different processes and match them with the best options from a–e below.

3.1

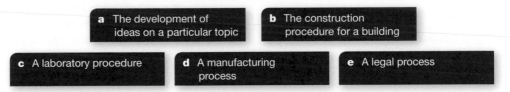

a The development of ideas on a particular topic

b The construction procedure for a building

c A laboratory procedure

d A manufacturing process

e A legal process

1b Work in pairs. Discuss which types of sequence or process are important to understand in your subject area.

1c Work in small groups. Think of things that a speaker can do in a spoken description of a process or sequence to deliver the information as clearly and effectively as possible. Make notes in the box below.

Elements of an effective process description
use clear signposting language

1d Listen to two different people describing the process in the flow chart below and decide whose description is more effective. Give reasons for your answer.

3.2

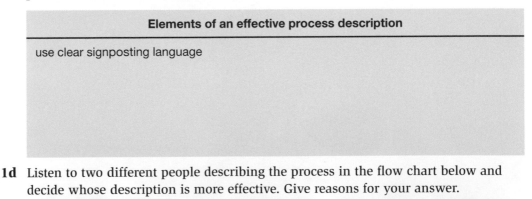

Secondary research of data since 1980 review → Categorize results → Interviews with 20 companies → Use information from interviews to create detailed questionnaires → Detailed questionnaires sent to 87 companies

1e Work in pairs and discuss your reasons.

2 Following an account of the development of ideas over time

> There is rarely complete agreement on ideas or theories about a particular topic. Knowledge of a subject develops and changes over time as more research is done, or competing ideas become more or less popular. Understanding the development of ideas can help you take a more critical approach to particular theories on a topic.

2a You are going to listen to a lecturer describing the historical development of ideas about the treatment of headaches. Before you listen, work in pairs and look at the different periods in the table below. Brainstorm ideas about how headaches may have been treated in each time and place. Write your ideas in the second column of the table.

Period	Approaches to treating headaches	
	Your ideas	Notes from listening
Ancient Egypt		
Ancient Rome		
19th century		
20th century		

3.3

2b Listen to the lecture. As you listen, take notes in the table above about the way headaches were treated in each of the different periods. Were any of your ideas correct?

2c Work in groups. Discuss how approaches to treating headaches have changed through time.

3 Following a description of a manufacturing process

3a In this section you will learn about the manufacturing process for a medicine. Before you begin, work in small groups and discuss these questions.

1 Do you ever take aspirin?

2 Do you know how most modern aspirin is made?

3b The diagram below illustrates the sequence by which aspirin is made (1–8). Work in pairs. Predict the order of the steps in the sequence (a–h) in the flow diagram below.

a Lubricant is added to the mixture and blended gently together.

b The ingredients are weighed separately.

~~**c** The tablets are tested for quality.~~

d The tablets are packaged on an assembly line.

e The ingredients are mixed and compressed.

~~**f** Air and lumps are removed from the compressed mixture by filtering.~~

g The tablets are labelled and a batch number and an expiry date are added to the container.

h The mixture is compressed into individual tablets.

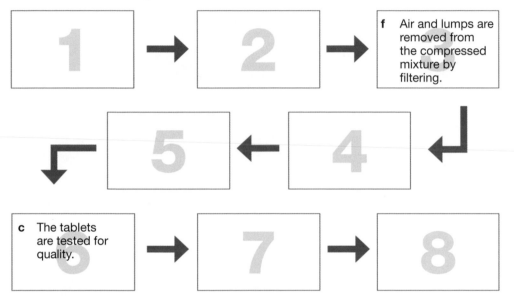

3c Listen to part of a lecture in which the lecturer explains the process in more detail. Check whether your prediction of the sequence was correct.

3.4

3d Compare your answers with a partner.

4 Following a description of a lab procedure

Understanding the steps in a lab procedure may be important not only for the success of the lab, but for your own safety as well.

4a You are going to listen to a demonstration of a lab experiment in which the instructor creates aspirin using the materials below. Before you begin, check that you understand the materials used in this stage of the experiment.

Materials				
test tube	acetyl chloride	beaker	salicylic acid	pyridine

4b Work in pairs. Try to predict the order of the steps in the first part of the procedure (a–e).

Step	Position in sequence
a Add 0.1 ml of acetyl chloride	
b Leave the mixture sitting in cold water for 15 minutes	
c Place 140 mg of salicylic acid in a test tube	1
d Add 0.1 ml of pyridine	
e Place the tube in a beaker of cold water and place it in the fume hood	

4c Listen to the first part of the demonstration and check that your sequence is correct.

3.5

4d A student has not listened very carefully to a series of instructions for the lab experiment, with some unfortunate consequences. Look at the list of problems that the student had, and decide the likely cause of the problem in each case.

Problem: 1 The student got irritated skin.

Problem: 2 The lab was filled with a terrible smell while the student was using the pyridine, and had to be evacuated for a while.

4e Work in pairs. Check that you understand what materials are used in the next section of the experiment. Then predict the order of the steps in the second part of the procedure.

Materials

Büchner flask   Büchner funnel   rubber tube   test tube   aspirator

Step	Position in sequence
a Set up the Büchner flask, funnel, pipe and aspirator	1
b Empty the crystals onto a piece of filter paper and leave them to dry	
c Shake the mixture	
d Pour the test tube mixture into the Büchner funnel and apply suction	
e Create a vacuum in the Büchner flask	
f Add 5 ml of water to the test tube	

4f Listen to the second part of the experiment. Check the sequence of steps.

3.6

4g Work in pairs. Look at the problem which another student had below. Discuss the possible reasons for the problem they had.

Problem: Water flowed into the Büchner flask and ruined the experiment.

4h Work in pairs. Predict the sequence of steps in the final part of the experiment.

Step	Position in sequence
Leave the solution to cool	
Heat the solution until the crystals dissolve	
Put the dry crystals into a beaker and add water	

3.7

4i Listen to the final part of the demonstration and check that the sequence of steps is correct.

4j Check your answers with a partner.

4k Work in pairs. Look at the problem below which another student had. Discuss the possible reasons for this problem.

Problem: The student added 30 millilitres of water to the crystals, then dissolved them by heating on a hotplate. They waited a very long time for the solution to cool, but no aspirin formed.

> **UNIT TASK** **Traditional, complementary and modern medicine**

The Unit 3 task is about traditional, complementary and modern medicine. At the end of each part, you will be asked to complete a stage of the task as follows:

Part A: Listen to an introduction on the topic.

Part B: Read a text about it.

Part C: Do some further research for relevant material.

Part D: Have a group discussion on the topic.

Part E: Write a report with one of these titles:

Assignment 1

A local health authority is planning to allocate some of its healthcare budget to the provision of complementary and alternative medicines. A number of doctors argue against this on the grounds that complementary medicines are not effective, saying that the money would be better spent on 'modern' healthcare. Write a recommendation report for the health authority to help them decide whether to use the budget for complementary medicine or not. Consider issues such as evidence for effectiveness, cost and public demand.

Assignment 2

According to the World Health Organization, over 80% of people in developing nations rely on traditional medicines for their healthcare.

At the same time, in developed nations there is a growing interest in complementary and traditional medicines, even though these nations already have modern healthcare systems. Write a report outlining trends in the use of traditional and complementary medicines in a country or region of your choice.

a Choose one of the assignment titles. Work with other students who have chosen the same assignment title as you. Briefly answer these questions about the assignment title.

Assignment 1

1 What are the two options that the assignment is asking you to consider?

2 Based on effectiveness, cost and demand, which of the two options do you tend to support right now? Explain your reasons.

Assignment 2

1 For this assignment title, do you need to make a strong recommendation in your report?

2 At the moment, which countries or regions are you interested in researching for the report? Explain your reasons.

b You are going to listen to a short general introduction to the use of different types of medical treatment. Before you listen, work in groups. Discuss these questions.

1 What is the difference between traditional and complementary treatments, and so-called 'modern' medicine?

2 How popular are traditional or complementary medicines in your own society?

3 What is your own opinion of traditional or non-scientific medical systems?

4 Have you ever used any traditional/complementary medical treatments? How satisfied were you with their results?

c Listen and take notes. Use these suggested topic headings to help you structure your notes.

3.8

Assignment 1

- Background
- Types of complementary medicines
- Advantages of complementary medicines
- Disadvantages of complementary medicines

Assignment 2

- Background
- Definitions
- Trends in use of traditional medicine in developing countries
- Reasons for these trends
- Trends in use of traditional or complementary medicine in developed nations
- Reasons for these trends

d Work in small groups again and compare your notes. Discuss how the information you heard relates to the assignment title you have chosen.

Go to the checklist on p.241 and read the tips relating to Unit 3 Part A.

1d Use your notes to complete the flow chart to show the sequence of stages in the development of a new medicine.

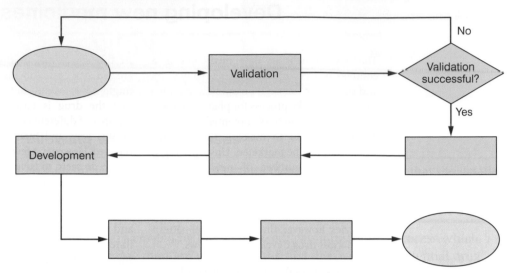

1e Compare your flow chart with a partner.

2 Interpreting process diagrams and flow charts

> Process diagrams and flow charts of different sorts are commonly used in many types of academic text.

2a Work in small groups. Brainstorm the benefits of using diagrams to represent processes visually. Make notes of your answers.

Notes

2b Share your ideas with the class.

2c Read this text, which gives more ideas about the benefits of representing processes in flow charts and diagrams. Add any more ideas from the text to your notes in 2a.

> Flow charts and process diagrams are used frequently in academic and certain types of technical writing. Some processes are so complicated that they can more easily be represented visually than by explaining them in text. Indeed, many people find that flow charts can help them to understand even fairly basic processes more easily by visualizing the steps rather than by trying to imagine them as they read. Representing ideas visually offers several more benefits to the reader than simply helping them to understand the order of steps, however. A flow chart should be able to show the relationship of certain parts of a process, as well as indicate where several different options are possible. Flow charts can help readers to critically analyze the process, helping them to identify potential weaknesses and judge whether a process is sensible or not.

2d Flow charts sometimes represent stages in a process through the use of different symbols. Work in pairs. Discuss what these symbols from the flow chart in 1d represent.

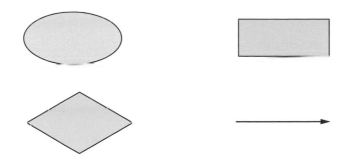

2e Use the information in the flow chart below to answer these questions.

1 In total, how many stages are there in the process?

2 How many decisions need to be made about what to do during the whole process?

3 When Phase 1 clinical trials begin, how confident can the drug developers be that the drug will eventually be put forward for registration?

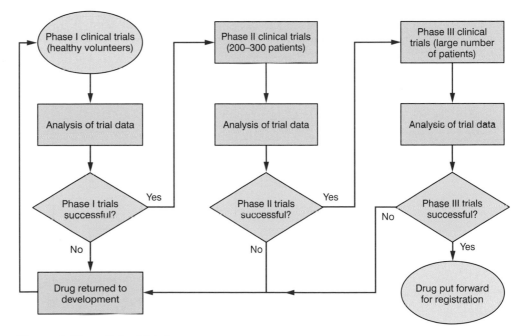

Figure 1: The clinical trials process

2f Compare your ideas with a partner.

3 Evaluating processes

3a The Wellco pharmaceutical company is planning to release a new shampoo treatment for dandruff. As part of the marketing, they have asked for a billboard advertising the shampoo. The text below explains the process by which the billboard advert will be planned and approved. Read the description of the billboard planning and approval process and annotate the flow chart.

Wellco's new dandruff control shampoo, 'Flakeze', will be released onto the market as an over-the-counter treatment in autumn next year. As part of the preparation for releasing the drug, a marketing campaign directly targeting consumers will be run throughout spring and summer of next year. As part of this campaign, Wellco's marketing department will produce billboard adverts to advertize the product. The following process will be followed for development and approval of the design:

1 Wellco's marketing director will draft a concept for the advert before passing it to the vice-director for marketing, who will make comments and then pass the draft concept on to the marketing team.

2 At this stage, the marketing team will create three or four improved draft versions, and present them to the marketing director for review. The director will either choose one of the improved drafts or recommend that the team create new drafts if none of the suggested ones is suitable.

3 After one of the designs has been approved, Wellco will hire the Benson and Knott advertising agency to develop a complete advert from Wellco's improved draft. After Benson and Knott's designers have completed a first full draft of the advert, they will pass it back to Wellco's marketing team for approval and suggestions.

4 If Wellco's team approves the design, Benson and Knott will go forward and create a complete final design for the advert. When the design has been finalized, it will be passed to Wellco.

5 The marketing team will meet with the vice-director of marketing to approve the advert design.

6 If they approve the final design, it will pass on to an executive meeting between the vice-director and director of marketing, where a final decision will be made about whether to use that advert.

7 If approval is given at this stage, Wellco will instruct Benson and Knott to begin creating the advert.

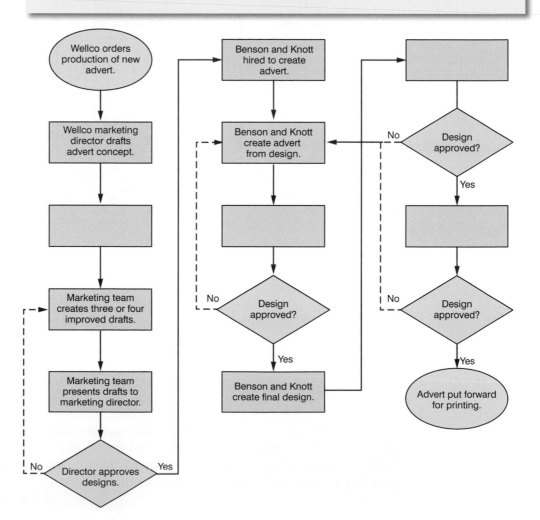

3b Check your answers with a partner. Then use the flow chart to evaluate the decision-making process by answering these questions.

   1 Are there any places where steps in the task are duplicated?

   2 Which parts of the process are likely to be most time consuming? Why?

   3 Is there any way that the process could be streamlined?

   4 Does anything seem to be missing from the process?

3c Work in pairs to create a flow chart of a streamlined decision-making process for Wellco.

3d Compare your ideas with another pair of students. Explain your reasons for the way you designed the process.

4   Critically analyzing reported statistics

> Numerical data and statistics can help to support claims made in a text, but they should not be accepted without question. The quality and reliability of any statistical information depend on the source of the information, the way it was analyzed, and how accurately it is reported to the reader.

4a You are going to read about the development of a new medicine for treating colds. Before you begin, work in pairs and discuss these questions.

   1 How often do you suffer from common colds?

   2 What are the typical symptoms of a cold?

   3 How long do common colds normally last for?

   4 What is the most effective treatment for a cold?

4b Work in pairs to complete the table.

Student A

Read the newspaper report and fill the first row of the table.

Student B

Read the abstract of the original research article and fill in the second row of the table.

(If you can't find the information you are looking for, just write 'not given' in the table.)

Data Source	Test subjects			Effects of Venalone		
	Age	Gender	Physical condition	After 24 hours	After 48 hours	After 5 days or more
Newspaper report						
Research article						

Student A:
Newspaper report

New drug cures colds in 24 hours

The dry throat, achiness and runny nose which signal the misery of a cold are a feeling familiar to everyone. Now, though, scientists in Sweden are offering sufferers almost instant relief with a newly developed drug which can cure a cold within 24 hours.

The researchers report that in clinical trials, 80% of test subjects who took the drug to treat colds had no symptoms after 24 hours. The study, which was conducted at the Stockholm Institute for Cold Research, revealed that sufferers were able to rid themselves of most major cold symptoms more quickly when treated with Venalone than with conventional treatments. An institute spokesperson said 'this is a very encouraging result. It is of course good news for our team, and is a very promising development for the millions of people who suffer the inconvenience of common colds every year.'

Student B:
Research article abstract

Viral respiratory tract infections (normally known as common colds) are a well-known source of irritation for most people. People infected with the common cold typically suffer symptoms including sore throats, coughing, increased nasal mucous, sneezing, as well as bodily aches and pains. Left without direct treatment, these symptoms will normally disappear within 7–10 days. Various treatments exist which are intended to alleviate the worst of the symptoms, rather than attempt any cure of the virus itself. In the present study, ten otherwise healthy males between the ages of 18 and 26 were exposed to cold viruses and then treated with the active ingredient in the compound marketed commercially as Venalone. After 24–48 hours, eight of the test subjects reported that they felt less pain overall, and rated their sense of well-being as 'improved'. Most of their symptoms had disappeared completely within five days. The other two subjects continued to display cold symptoms for approximately one more week. The results tentatively indicate a slight positive effect on all cold symptoms in sufferers as a result of being treated with Venalone.

4c Check your answers with a partner.

4d Work in pairs. Discuss these questions.

1 According to the report in the newspaper, how effective is the medicine?

2 What evidence does the newspaper report give to support the claim that the medicine is effective?

3 Does the newspaper report describe the findings of the original research accurately?

4 From the research article abstract, how certain can you be that Venalone is an effective cure for colds?

5 Were there any weaknesses in this study that might make you less certain that Venalone is an effective treatment for colds?

4e Work in pairs. Make a list of questions that you could ask yourself to think critically about when reading reported statistics.

Questions to ask yourself when reading reported statistics
e.g. what is the original source of the information?

> **UNIT TASK**   **Traditional, complementary and modern medicine**

In this unit task, you will read more about trends in the use of traditional and complementary medicines to help you build your background knowledge as you carry out your own research on the subject.

Read and take notes on the text below. As you read, bear in mind the assignment title that you have chosen to write about, and consider how this information relates specifically to that title.

Traditional and complementary medicine use

Hobson, S. (2010). Traditional and complementary medicine use. *Complementary Medicine Bulletin*, *15*(4), 1157–1161.

Introduction

Medical care can be divided into two broad approaches: so-called conventional medicine – sometimes labelled 'scientific', 'modern', or even 'Western' medicine – is that based on empirical research and development of medicines and therapeutic techniques designed to treat specific illnesses or conditions in a patient. A contrasting approach can be found in what are known as 'traditional' medical systems (TM). These are defined by the World Health Organization (WHO) as:

The sum total of knowledge, skills and practices based on the theories, beliefs and experiences indigenous to different cultures that are used to maintain health, as well as to prevent, diagnose, improve or treat physical and mental illnesses (WHO, 2008).

TM systems include the use of herbs and minerals, spiritual healing techniques, massage, and promotion of a generally healthy individual rather than using medical science to target a specific illness or problem. It has famously been estimated that 80% of all people in developing nations around the world rely on traditional medicines for their healthcare (Bannerman et al., 1983). Most nations and cultures have their own traditional healthcare practices, though some, such as traditional Chinese medicine and Indian Ayurveda, have become popular in the world outside their countries of origin. When traditional medicines are adopted in other cultures and used alongside orthodox 'scientific' medicines, they are often known as complementary and alternative medicine (CAM). In many developed nations in recent years there has been increasing interest in CAM based on traditional knowledge from other cultures, possibly as a result of the desire for a system of healthcare which sees 'health' as more than just 'treating illnesses'.

Trends in TM/CAM use

TM/CAM are widely used throughout the world. The WHO notes that not only is this significant for health in many regions of the world, but it is also of economic importance (2002, p.1). One estimate of annual sales of medicines in Malaysia puts spending on conventional medicine at $300 million, compared to $500 million for TM/CAM; in Canada, annual out-of pocket spending on TM/CAM has been estimated at $2.4 billion (Health Canada, 2001); in the UK, also, an estimated £1.6 billion ($2.4 billion) is spent annually on non-conventional medical treatments (House of Lords, 2000). These figures are remarkable, particularly given that all three nations have well-funded, staffed and equipped conventional healthcare systems.

Reasons for choosing TM/CAM

Reasons for using non-conventional treatments differ between developing and developed nations, but also between socio-economic groups within nations.

In developing countries, the decision to use TM may be due to considerations of 'accessibility and affordability' (WHO, 2002, p.2), also because there may be long traditions within cultures that tend to make these systems preferred; the 1978 Alma Ata declaration recognized the need to formalize traditional approaches to medicine in societies that had strong cultures of traditional medical care, and where issues of cost and accessibility might mean that a healthcare system based solely on Western medicine might put effective healthcare out of reach for the poor.

This difference is evident in the ratio of traditional practitioners to population compared to conventional medical staff: in Ghana, for instance, there is an estimated ratio of one traditional healer for every 400 people, compared to one conventionally trained doctor for every 12,000 people (Tsey, 1997). Similar figures are reported by Mhame (2000, cited in WHO, 2002, p.12), who found between 200 and 400 traditional healers per person in Tanzania. The availability of conventionally trained physicians throughout large parts of Asia and sub-Saharan Africa is somewhere between five and 20 per 10,000 people (WHO, 2010, p.114).

In the developing world, cost may be a significant factor in the use of TM. Conventional anti-malarial tablets in Ghana, Kenya and Mali may cost 'several dollars', even though per capita out-of-pocket health expenditure typically comes to just $6 a year (WHO, 2002, p.13); costs such as these put these medicines out of reach for many.

However, it would give a false picture to portray TM use in the developing world as stemming solely from poverty. More economically well-off members of society, particularly in cities, may often be better able to access and pay for conventional Western medicines, or adopt a 'mixed' approach of using Western medicine for some things, and local traditional medicine for others. Such a 'pluralistic' approach to medical care is widespread in many societies (Bodeker, 2001), though of course in order to have the luxury of choice one must also have enough money to pay for it in the first place.

In developed nations which already have well-established and functioning conventional health systems, it might seem odd that there is growing interest in CAM, though it is likely that 'factors other than tradition and cost are at work' (WHO, 2002, p.14). A number of reasons have been advanced for this, notably concern about side effects in conventional medicine, questioning of the principles of scientific approaches to medicine, and changing values (ibid). A 1999 BBC-commissioned survey of 1,204 people in the UK found that the top three reasons for using CAM were: that it helped or relieved a specific condition; that respondents 'just like it'; and that they find it relaxing. However, interestingly enough, one other reason was referral by conventional doctors (Ernst & White, 2000).

Astin (1998) has claimed that the most significant predictors of CAM use in developed nations are high income, high education and chronic poor health, and that users tend to turn to these medicines because they match their own lifestyles and values.

Safety and efficacy

Despite the extensive growth of TM/CAM use, there remains considerable, and often heated, debate about the safety and clinical effectiveness of many non-conventional treatments when compared with modern conventional medicine. There is widespread doubt among many professionals working within the conventional medical field that TM/CAM treatments have any positive medical effect at all, with many expressing 'frank disbelief' about their supposed benefits (WHO, 2002, p.2). This becomes more of an issue than simply wasting money on ineffective cures when patients opt for TM/CAM treatments for serious medical conditions, thus delaying treatment with clinically proven, and potentially life-saving, conventional treatments. There is strong demand among those working within the conventional medical system for TM/CAM treatments to be rigorously tested for safety and efficacy, in the same manner as modern Western treatments are. Nevertheless, while it is certainly true that rigorous and extensive clinical evidence for the efficacy of many TM/CAM treatments is lacking, there is nevertheless a small body of research which suggests that certain of these treatments, notably acupuncture and particular herbal remedies, are effective.

Nevertheless, in the absence of an extensive and conclusive body of clinical evidence, there remains strong opposition even to these therapies among the conventional medical community, often citing concerns about safety. It has been claimed that herbal remedies available for over-the-counter treatment often contain unsafe levels of contaminants such as mercury and arsenic (Garvey et al., 2001). There are also concerns that there are no standard methods or training for TM/CAM, which can lead to inconsistent application and potentially harmful dosages or conflicts with chemical drugs (Boullata & Nace, 2000). The regulation of TM/CAM health systems, in terms of safety and efficacy, as well as practitioner training and drug registration, will be central to future strategies for the successful integration of these medical techniques into national health policies.

References

Astin, J.A. (1998). Why Patients use Alternative Medicine. Results of a National Survey. *The Journal of the American Medical Association, 279,* 1548–1553.

....

Bannerman, R.B., Buton, J. & Wen-Chieh, C. (1983). *Traditional medicine and health care coverage.* Geneva: World Health Organization.

....

Bodeker G. (2001). Lessons on integration from the developing world's experience. *The British Medical Journal, 322,* 164–167.

....

Boullata, J.I., & Nace, A.M. (2000). Safety Issues with Herbal Medicine. *Pharmacotherapy, 20*(3). 257–269. doi: 10.1592/phco.20.4.257.34886

....

Ernst, E., & White, A. (2000). The BBC Survey of Complementary Medicine Use in the UK. *Complementary Therapies in Medicine, 8,* 32–36.

....

Garvey, G. J., Hahn, G., Lee, R. V. & Harbison, R. D. (2001). Heavy metal hazards of Asian traditional remedies. *International Journal of Environmental Health Research, 11*(1), 63–71. doi:10.1080/09603120020019656

....

Health Canada. (2001). *Perspectives on Alternative and Complementary Health Care: a collection of papers prepared for Health Canada.* Ottawa: Health Canada.

....

House of Lords Select Committee on Science and Technology. (2000). *Sixth report: Complementary and Alternative Medicine.* Retrieved from http://www.publications.parliament.uk/pa/ld199900/ldselect/ldsctech/123/12301.htm

....

Tsey, K. (1997). Traditional medicine in contemporary Ghana: A public policy analysis. *Social Science & Medicine, 45*(7), 1065–1074. doi: 10.1016/S0277-9536(97)00034-8

Conclusion

TM/CAM are a broad collection of approaches to medical care, including some well-established systems which are widely regarded to have proven effectiveness, such as traditional Chinese medicine, and other more controversial practices, such as homeopathy or therapeutic prayer, for which clinical evidence of medical effectiveness is lacking. TM/CAM are widely used throughout the world. In many nations they have formed the core approach to medical care for hundreds or even thousands of years, and there is strong evidence to suggest that their use is growing in developed nations which have otherwise functioning 'conventional' medical systems. In developing regions, it is a potentially valuable healthcare resource due to problems of cost and access to modern medical treatment. Nevertheless, in order to develop the potential of TM/CAM, and overcome strong resistance among conventional medical professionals, further studies of efficacy and safety are required.

World Health Organization. (2002). *WHO Traditional Medicine Strategy 2002–2005*. Geneva: World Health Organization.

World Health Organization. (2008). *Traditional Medicine*. Retrieved from http://www.who.int/mediacentre/factsheets/fs134/en/

World Health Organization. (2010). *World Health Statistics 2010*. Geneva: World Health Organization

Go to the checklist on p.241. Look again at the tips relating to Unit 3 Part A and tick (✓) those you have used in your studies. Read the tips relating to Unit 3 Part B.

Part C   Investigating

By the end of Part C you will be able to:

- draw conclusions from data
- deal with sources of uncertainty
- avoid absolute terms
- protect your position through citation
- use cautious language for your own claims.

1   Drawing conclusions from data

> Data gives your audience information about your research findings, and helps to support your claims. However, it would be incorrect to say that any data proves that something is definitely true. It is quite likely that different people will interpret the same data in different ways.

1a Read the three sources below (A–C) about the status of complementary medicine in England. Answer these questions.

1 Which types of complementary medicine are well known and trusted in the UK?

2 Which types of complementary medicine are controversial?

3 In the UK, who tends to use complementary medicine more – men or women?

4 What age groups tend to use complementary medicine the most?

A

Recent decades have shown a growing interest among the public for complementary medicines (Fulder, 1988, p.15). If the mainstream medical system is one which is based on a scientific, empirical approach to drug development and medical procedures, then complementary medicines are those which are not usually offered within the mainstream medical system. Complementary medicines encompass a wide range of different treatments, some of them ancient and traditional – such as the use of well-known herbal treatments, or long-established Chinese or Indian Ayurvedic medicine, both of which enjoy widespread public acceptance – and newer and more controversial treatments such as homeopathy or radionics. This group of medical practices is sometimes collectively known as complementary and alternative medicine (CAM). The distinction is important: alternative medicines are those which are to some extent in opposition to mainstream modern medicine; supporters of alternative medical systems claim that they function as complete alternatives to the modern mainstream medical system. The term complementary medicine, however, suggests a different approach to medical care, in which it is recognized that non-mainstream medical treatments cannot entirely replace, or in many cases even match,

the effectiveness of modern medical techniques and drugs, but that they do offer certain benefits which are unavailable in the modern medical system. In the UK until relatively recently, it has been difficult to obtain reliable data about the numbers of people choosing to use CAM treatments. However, since the late 1990s a number of studies have provided some insight both into the numbers of people choosing CAM, and their reasons for doing so. One recent study of CAM use in England estimated that nearly 47% of English citizens would use some form of CAM in the course of their lifetime (Thomas et al., 2001, p.5). People appear to turn to CAM remedies, even where a modern medical system is available, for a variety of reasons, though one of the most common reasons appears to be that people turned to CAM after treatments with mainstream medicine proved unsatisfactory. Interestingly, many of the reasons for using CAM were not directly medical, which supports the idea that CAM treatments deal more with well-being rather than the direct treatment of specific illnesses; some of these non-medical reasons included respondents claiming that they used CAM products because they had been given them as gifts, or simply for a treat 'in order to feel good'.

B Table 1: Gender differences in use of complementary medicine in the UK.

Age	Male (% of sample)	Female (% of sample)	Both sexes (% of sample)
16–24	4.1	6.8	5.5
25–44	12.1	10.6	11.3
45–54	17.7	11.6	14.0
55–64	4.4	10.4	7.6
65–74	7.7	13.7	10.8
75+	7.4	6.7	6.9
Total	9.8	10.3	10.0

Based on a sample size of 1,786 UK adults.

Source: Thomas and Coleman, 2004

C Table 2: Estimated proportion of adult population receiving complementary medicine treatment during lifetime.

Treatment type	Estimated use over lifetime (% of population)
Acupuncture	7.0
Chiropractic	10.3
Homeopathic	5.7
Medical herbalism	4.4
Hypnotherapy	3.1
Osteopathy	13.0
Reflexology	5.4
Aromatherapy	8.2
Purchasing over-the-counter homeopathic treatments	14.6
Purchasing over-the-counter herbal treatments	31.4
Use at least one of the treatments listed above	46.6

Based on a sample size of 2,669 adults in England

Source: Thomas et al., 2001.

1b Check your answers with a partner.

1c Work in pairs. Discuss whether you agree with these claims about the growth of complementary medicine. Use data from all three sources in 1a to help support your ideas.

   1 The growth of complementary medicine in England is due to dissatisfaction with side effects associated with modern medicine.

   2 People are willing to trust complementary medicine because of the belief that the techniques are ancient and trusted.

   3 People are turning to complementary medicine because it is a cheaper alternative to modern medicine.

   4 It is likely that similar results would be found in other areas of the UK and other Western nations.

1d Read these two texts by different authors and answer these questions. Give reasons to support your opinions.

   1 To what extent do you agree with the first author's position (text A)?

   2 To what extent do you agree with the second author's position (text B)?

   3 Do you have any different or original ideas of your own to explain the rising popularity of complementary medicine?

A

A great deal has been written recently about the growing popularity of alternative medical treatments – those that eschew rigorous scientific testing in favour of vague explanations based on 'traditional' knowledge. In fact, the supposed popularity of complementary and alternative medicine (CAM) is itself illusory: the data indicates that the numbers of people who choose to use these therapies are, in fact, tiny.

Only very small numbers of the population in England, and presumably the entire UK and beyond, actually use individual CAM treatments. According to Thomas et al. (2001), this is only about 10% of the population for all types of CAM treatments. For both sexes its use is mainly found in the 45–54 age group, which suggests that small numbers of people turn to CAM in desperation after years of unsuccessfully trying conventional treatments. Despite claims that demand for CAM is widespread (see for instance Fulder, 1988; Thomas et al., 2001), the figures indicate only a very small number of people are actually willing to trust their health to this confused assortment of New Age rubbish.

B

CAM treatments enjoy widespread popularity in the UK. As early as 1988 Fulder observed a growing appetite for access to alternative treatments. As the data in Table 2 above indicates, people interested in receiving CAM in England can choose from a wide menu of alternative treatments, so it is unsurprising that as many as 10% of the population use CAM treatments annually. With an estimated 47% of the English population likely to turn to CAM treatments at some point in the course of their lives (Thomas et al., 2001, p.5), it is perhaps fair to say that the medical system in England (if not the UK as a whole), is one which fairly balances both scientific, modern, medical therapies with non-conventional approaches to treatment.

1e Read the statements in the table and tick (✓) the correct column, Agree or Disagree.

Statement	Agree	Disagree
1 You can be certain that what you read is correct if it is written by an expert.		
Reason:		
2 You should not automatically accept that claims are true just because they are supported by data.		
Reason:		
3 You cannot trust any data you read.		
Reason:		
4 You should not assume that your own conclusions about what data means are true.		
Reason:		
5 You should question where the data came from, who collected it, and how it was gathered.		
Reason:		

1f Work in small groups and check your answers. Give reasons for your ideas.

2 Dealing with sources of uncertainty

There is always some uncertainty about research results and data: we can never be completely certain that the data accurately reveals what we think it does, and therefore if the conclusions we draw from this data are reasonable. The way a writer deals with this uncertainty affects the quality of their claims and writing. Good academic writing does not ignore possible sources of uncertainty in data; instead, it acknowledges that the uncertainties are there and helps the reader to understand how reliable the data is.

2a Read this text about different sources of uncertainty in research. As you read, make a note of the different sources of uncertainty which the author mentions.

Uncertainty is a fact of life in academic research. When academic writers make claims, they inevitably do so knowing that the claims themselves are based only on evidence which might be true. This uncertainty comes from a variety of different sources. Firstly, most claims are based on research data, and this data is only as strong as the methods that were used to collect it, so a study which used a flawed method may well produce data which is inaccurate or distorted. Even a study in which the method is sound may be limited by other factors such as the number of people interviewed or measurements taken. If, for instance, you want to find out what proportion of the UK population have tried Chinese medicine, you cannot realistically interview all of them, so you must rely on a sample which you hope is representative of the population as a whole. This immediately means that you can't be sure that the results are perfectly accurate.

Uncertainty can also creep in when you analyze data. It may be that you accidentally misinterpret data as suggesting something that is not, in fact, the case. You cannot be certain that your own interpretation, or that of others, is entirely accurate; you can only try to make sure that it is as accurate as possible. Writers can also run into trouble when using data or claims from other authors to support their own work. The writers and researchers whose work you are using may themselves have used data which is inconclusive, or they may in turn have interpreted the data incorrectly. It is also, unfortunately, the case that some sources of information deliberately misrepresent the data that they use in order to persuade their readers to accept their claims. As a consequence, academic writing tends to be viewed with suspicion if it makes claims which are overly certain, or does not appear to acknowledge the possibility that the viewpoint it puts it forward may be inaccurate. The best academic writing instead carefully indicates how certain the author is about the information they are using, and the claims they base on it.

Notes
e.g. research method might be flawed

2b Work in pairs. Look at this information about a study of the use of herbal treatments in the UK. Is there anything about the method used for the study that might make the findings less certain?

Author:	Burke, P.
Study carried out:	2003
Published:	2004
Method:	Postal questionnaires about use of herbs were mailed to 4,000 people. The respondents were asked to estimate how much they thought they had spent on herbal medicines in the past year. The results were used to make an estimate of total expenditure for the UK population.
Response rate:	55% (2,200) of the respondents replied. Of that number, 80% (1,760) were women.
Findings:	Respondents spent an average of £27.5 on herbal treatments in the UK in 2003. Average yearly spending on herbal treatments in the UK was estimated at £47 million a year.

2c A student has written a description of the research in 2b. Read the passage below and answer the questions to help you decide how well this student has acknowledged different sources of uncertainty about the data.

1 To what extent do you accept the claim that herbal medicine is used 'by all cultures in the world'?

2 To what extent do you accept the claim that it is 'clear' that herbal treatments are popular?

3 Does the claim 'People in the UK spent … £27.50 each on herbal medicines in 2003' accurately reflect Burke's findings? What is the difference between saying 'People in the UK' and 'Respondents'?

4 What is the difference between these two sentences?

  a Burke shows that total spending on herbal remedies in the UK is £47 million a year.

  b Burke estimates that total spending on herbal remedies in the UK is £47 million a year.

5 Which of the two sentences in question 4 would be the more accurate description of Burke's findings?

6 To what extent do you accept the writer's claim that herbal treatments 'clearly … remain highly popular among people in the UK'?

> Herbal medicine, the use of active properties in plants and flowers for medical use, is one of the most ancient forms of medical treatment, and is still practised to this day by all cultures in the world.
>
> Today, people rely on herbal medicines to cure a wide variety of ailments. The popularity of herbal treatments is clear from the amount that is spent on them every year. In the UK, where a modern medical system exists which is free for all citizens, many people still choose to pay for herbal medicines out of their own pockets; People in the UK spent an average of £27.50 each on herbal medicines in 2003 (Burke, 2004). Burke shows that total spending on herbal remedies in the UK is £47 million a year, either bought as part of a course of treatment with a qualified herbalist, or purchased as an over-the-counter remedy. Clearly, then, herbal treatments remain highly popular among people in the UK.

2d Check your answers with a partner and suggest improvements to the description of the research.

> There are three ways to acknowledge sources of uncertainty in your writing:
>
> 1 Avoid making statements which use absolute terms.
>
> 2 Use citations to other authors in a way that acknowledges uncertainty in their work.
>
> 3 Use cautious language for your own claims.
>
> These three techniques are sometimes referred to collectively as hedging – using careful statements to qualify claims that you make. One of the best ways to improve your ability to use hedging in your own writing is to read academic texts widely and observe how the authors use hedging in their own work.

3 Avoiding absolute terms

> Extreme positions on a topic are expressed in absolute terms. They often make categorical claims about what is true which are easily challenged, or overly general statements which are unlikely to apply to everything for which the claim is made. For example, in each of the sentences below, the author uses absolute terms.
>
> - The Western approach to medicine is the most effective.
> - Everybody can benefit from using traditional medicine.

3a You are going to read two versions (a and b) of three texts (1–3). Read the texts and compare the use of absolute terms and hedging language. Complete the table. Compare the use of absolute terms and hedging language in the two texts below (a and b) and complete the table.

Words/expressions to avoid	Useful words/expressions
all	many

1

a India, like all countries, has a medical system based on the modern 'scientific' approach to healthcare. This is the 'Western' system. The modern Western medical system relies on treating patients with high-tech equipment and expensive drugs manufactured by multinational pharmaceutical companies. This system is only available to the rich; no ordinary Indians can afford to use it. Furthermore, people now understand that modern Western medicine is ineffective. However, because it is the dominant system promoted by the government, people only use it because they have no choice.

b Like many other nations, India's medical system is based on the modern 'scientific' approach to healthcare (sometimes known as the 'Western' system). The modern Western medical system tends to rely on treating patients with high-tech equipment and expensive drugs manufactured by multinational pharmaceutical companies. Consequently, it is limited to those who can afford to pay. Many ordinary Indians cannot afford to do this. A further issue with modern medicine in India is the awareness that it is not effective in every situation. However, as it is the dominant system promoted by the government, many Indians feel forced to use it because they have no cheaper or more effective option.

2

---

a In the past, most people visiting an acupuncturist did so because they were suffering from muscular or joint pain. The proportion of people visiting acupuncturists for this reason has declined in recent years, while the proportion of people visiting an acupuncturist for other treatments (e.g. psychological, quitting smoking, or general health treatments) has risen. This is due to the fact that acupuncture has become better known around the world, and everybody knows that it can be used for a range of different treatments. In the UK, for instance, with the ban on public smoking in 2007, and high tobacco prices, everyone wants to quit, and acupuncture is the most effective method for stopping: as a result, acupuncturists have seen large rises in the number of smokers visiting them.

b Historically, most visits to acupuncturists were for the treatment of muscular or joint pain. However, the proportion of people visiting acupuncturists for this reason has declined in recent years, while the proportion of people visiting an acupuncturist for other treatments (e.g. psychological, quitting smoking, or general health treatments) has risen. This may be due to increasing public awareness of acupuncture; more people are now aware of the different range of medical problems that it can be used to treat. In the UK, for instance, with the ban on public smoking in 2007, and high tobacco prices, increasing numbers of smokers are looking for help to quit, and acupuncture is seen as being one effective method for doing this: as a result, many acupuncturists have seen an increase in the number of smokers visiting them.

3

---

a Studies of acupuncture all show that women like to visit acupuncturists more than men (for instance Macpherson et al., 2006; Thomas et al., 1988). This is because women always visit doctors more than men. The survey shows that the majority of people going to acupuncturists are between the ages of 35 and 70. Clearly, this is because everybody develops health problems as they get older, so they need to visit the doctor more often.

b Several recent studies of patients' reasons for visiting acupuncturists indicate that women tend to visit acupuncturists more than men (for instance Macpherson et al., 2006; Thomas et al., 1988). One possible reason for this is that women tend to visit doctors of all types more often than men do. Another finding of the survey is that the majority of people visiting acupuncturists are between the ages of 35 and 70. This may have something to do with increased health problems in this age group.

3b Work in pairs. Review your answers to 2d. Have you used suitably cautious language?

4 Protecting your position through citation

> Another way that writers deal with and express uncertainty is to refer to other people's work in ways that suggest their own opinions about it.

4a A student is writing an essay about traditional medicine. He wants to give some information from a source (Jones, 2009) about the Persian physician Avicenna.

Work in pairs. Discuss which of the three sentences on p.163 (a–c) shows that the student is most certain that the information about Avicenna is correct. Then identify which of the three sentences shows that the student is least certain about the information.

a The medieval Persian physician Avicenna (Ibn Sina) was the first person to suggest the use of clinical trials for medicines (Jones, 2009, p.14).

b According to Jones (2009, p.14), clinical trials for medicines were first suggested by the medieval Persian physician Avicenna.

c Jones (2009, p.14) notes that the medieval Persian physician Avicenna was the first person to suggest the use of clinical trials for medicines.

4b Work in pairs. Tick (✓) the correct column on the table according to whether the author completely agrees that (C) the information is true, accepts (A) that the information is probably true, or leaves room for doubt (D) that the information is true.

	C	A	D
1 80% of people in developing countries rely on traditional medicine (WHO, 2008).			
2 According to Saito (2007), traditional medicines are significantly less effective than so-called 'modern' or Western medicine.			
3 Wilson and Lavelle (2003) have proved that most herbal treatments are at least as effective as other drugs in treating common colds.			
4 Nutwell (2006) claims that homeopathic remedies, despite the lack of clinical evidence, are effective.			

4c Compare the two texts below, which give information about the use of herbal medicines in the UK. As you read, underline the phrases that each author has used to introduce citations.

1

Herbal medicines are used widely within the UK (Benson et al., 2009). Indeed, as a recent study by Cox (2008) indicates, rising annual sales of herbal medicines suggest that their popularity is on the increase. This popularity is probably due to a number of factors: low price compared to the costs of conventional drugs (Cox, ibid); a popular notion that herbal treatments have fewer side effects (Lasky et al., 2005); and a growing interest in spiritual, traditional or 'holistic' approaches to staying healthy which are not typically offered in the mainstream medical system (Campbell & Ho, 2008). It seems, then, that people turn to herbal medicines and other similar treatments both because of typical consumer behaviour (sensitivity to cost and comparison of different products) as well as a rising attraction to 'alternative' lifestyle choices in the UK at large.

According to Quinn (2008), approximately 35% of the UK population will use herbal remedies of some sort during their lifetime, either by visiting a herbal practitioner or by purchasing over-the-counter remedies in a shop. Numerous explanations have been given for the apparent popularity of these remedies. Cox (2008) notes that the costs of herbal remedies are often far lower than conventional drugs (both in terms of monetary cost, and the time spent visiting a doctor to receive a prescription). However, there may be other factors involved besides cost. According to Fuller (1999), herbal remedies have far fewer side effects than mainstream treatments. One study by Ponzio and Stewart (2004) suggests that this benign view of herbal medicines is widespread among the general public, who may therefore be more inclined to choose herbal medicines to treat less serious conditions. A further possibility for the widespread reliance on herbal medicines is suggested by Campbell and Ho (2008), who claim that herbal medicines fit in with a growing interest in 'alternative' lifestyle choices in the UK. There is a growing interest in spirituality, alternative philosophies and fascination with ancient healing systems from other nations such as India and China, and herbalism naturally falls into that category of lifestyle choices.

4d Work in pairs. Consider the two texts in 4c again and discuss these questions.

1 Which of the two authors seems more certain overall about the information they are presenting?

2 How certain does the author of the first text seem about the claim that herbal medicines are widely used in the UK?

3 To what extent do you accept the first author's claims as true? What could the writer do to help persuade you that these claims are likely to be true?

4e Work in pairs. Read the texts below and decide how certain each author is about the information that they are presenting.

1

Leeches have been used medicinally since ancient times (Fields, 1991). A variety of leeches have been employed for medical purposes, though the most common species is *Hirudo medicinalis* (Eldor et al., 1996, p.202). The application of leeches was known in many cultures, where they were traditionally used for removing 'excessive' blood, but also for pain relief and the treatment of a number of related physical ailments. Leeches were still employed in considerable numbers as recently as the early 1800s: according to Adams (1988), St Bartholomew's Hospital in London used over 97,000 leeches in the year 1832, while in Paris between the years 1829 and 1836, between five and six million leeches were applied to patients. However, with the development of alternative, scientific medical techniques, leeches increasingly fell out of favour until eventually they were dismissed as a 'discredited medical relic of the past' (Eldor et al., 1996, p.201).

Recently, however, Western medical practitioners have reassessed the therapeutic benefits of using leeches. Wells et al. (1993) point out that evidence suggests that medical leeching can be an effective procedure in some cases. Leeches have been employed in the replantation of severed fingers and toes (Wells et al., ibid); leech saliva has been used in treatments for heart conditions (Eldor et al., 1996); and leeches have been applied in the traditional way (bleeding) to the knees of patients suffering from arthritis, where there is evidence that they were effective in treating pain (Michaelsen et al., 2003).

There are a number of reasons for this revival: partially it is, as Wells et al. suggest, because of a re-examination by medical practitioners of their uses. However, Eldor et al. (ibid) also suggest that this is due to a resurgence of interest in natural and alternative therapies.

There is little public awareness of the debt that modern medicine owes to the work of medieval Arab and Persian scholars. In the 9th to 11th centuries, a number of prominent physicians and philosophers were influential in the development of modern medical theories. Notable scholars included the Iraqi polymath Abū Yusūf al-Kindī (known in the West as Al Kindus, 801–873); the Persian scholars Abu Ali Ibn-e-Sina (Avicenna, 980–1037); Abu Bakr Al-Râzi (Rhazes, 865–925), and Ali Ebn Al-Abbas-al-Majusi (Haly Abbas, 949–982 AD) (Porter, 1997). The contribution of the Persian scholars is often overlooked because they have often been grouped together with other 'Arab' scholars as a consequence of the fact that many Persian medical texts tended to be written in the Arabic language (Campbell, 2000).

This group of scholars had considerable influence. Avicenna, frequently considered the greatest of all the medieval physicians, is credited with being the first person to suggest the testing of medicines with clinical trials. In the medical school of the University of Brussels, lectures based on Avicenna's texts were still delivered until the early 1900s (Gorji & Ghadiri, 2002). Though there are clearly elements of their work, Avicenna's included, which time has shown to be erroneous, a great many fundamental discoveries and practices can be attributed to them.

Medieval Persian medicine synthesized the knowledge and practices of ancient Greece, India, China and Egypt. However, as Gorji and Ghadiri have observed, medieval Persian physicians did not just follow older traditional practices, but also made valuable contributions to medical knowledge, introducing 'many new scientific theories' (ibid, 510).

5 Using cautious language for your own claims

> When you make claims in your own writing, you should acknowledge uncertainty about whether the claims are completely true or not by using cautious language.

5a Read the three pairs of texts on p.166 and decide which text in each pair uses the most appropriate language.

5b Check your answers with a partner.

5c Complete the table with language from the texts.

Words/expressions to avoid	Useful words/expressions to show caution

1

a Pharmaceutical manufacturing capacity is very restricted: over 92% of all new drug development takes place in the so-called high-income countries (WHO, 2004, p.5). The share of drugs manufactured in the poor and middle-income countries is decreasing all the time, because the development of new drugs is a slow and costly process, requiring funding and high technology which are beyond the means of all but the largest corporations in the wealthy industrialized nations. This concentration of manufacturing capacity in just a few organizations, however, has serious consequences. The drug companies focus on developing only those medicines which they expect to be profitable, and having made them they protect them with commercial patents and charge high prices for them, even though other non-brand medicines are just as good. As a result, people in poorer countries are unable to get access to the best medicines because they are too expensive.

b Pharmaceutical manufacturing capacity is very restricted. According to the WHO (2004, p.5), over 92% of all new drug development takes place in the so-called high-income countries. The share of drugs manufactured in the poor and middle-income countries has decreased somewhat in recent years. It seems likely that this is because the development of new drugs tends to be a slow and costly process, requiring funding and high technology which are beyond the means of all but the largest corporations in the wealthy industrialized nations. This apparent concentration of manufacturing capacity in just a few organizations, however, may have serious consequences. Evidence suggests that the drug companies focus on developing only those medicines which they expect to be profitable, and having made them they protect them with commercial patents. Medicines manufactured by the largest pharmaceutical corporations tend to be considerably more expensive than non-brand medicines, even though these medicines may be equally effective. As a result, it is difficult for people in poorer countries to get access to the best medicines, at least in part because they are too expensive.

2

a Every two years the World Health Organization produces a list of essential medicines. These medicines are the ones which the WHO determines are absolutely critical for the treatment all the medical conditions which can be influenced or cured by medicine. The latest list identifies only 300 to 400 medicines as 'essential'. However, there are a large number of other medicines which, though effective, may not be essential. Interestingly, a large percentage of the medicines sold in the developing world by major pharmaceutical firms are not in the WHO's 'essential' category. This has contributed to claims that the major pharmaceutical firms tend to ignore Third World health problems.

b Every two years the World Health Organization produces a list of essential medicines. These medicines are the ones which are absolutely critical for the treatment all the medical conditions which can be influenced or cured by medicine. The latest list proves that only 300 to 400 medicines are 'essential'. However, there are many, many more medicines which, though effective, are not essential. Interestingly, a lot of the medicines sold in the developing world by major pharmaceutical firms are non-essential. This shows that major pharmaceutical corporations ignore Third World health problems.

3

a One study by the WHO shows that 50% of all medicines in low- and middle-income nations are used inappropriately. The reasons for this are: improper advertising of drugs directly to consumers, creating demand for drugs among patients; lack of training for doctors and nurses; and commercial pressure from pharmaceutical companies. Another reason is lack of access to critical information about the dosage and use of the drugs.

b One study by the WHO indicates that 50% of all medicines in low- and middle-income nations are used inappropriately. This may be due to several different factors: improper advertising of drugs directly to consumers, creating demand for drugs among patients; lack of training for doctors and nurses; and commercial pressure from pharmaceutical companies. Another possible reason may be lack of access to critical information about the dosage and use of the drugs.

> **UNIT TASK**   **Traditional, complementary and modern medicine**

Later in this unit you will participate in a discussion and then write a short report on your chosen medicines assignment title. You have already started gathering information about the topic from the notes you took in the listening (unit task Part A), as well as the text in Part B.

a   Look closely at the source which you read in unit task Part B again. Think about how certain the author is about the information in the claims they are making. Complete the table below by deciding whether the author completely agrees that the information is true, accepts that the information is probably true, or leaves room for doubt about whether the information is true.

Main idea of text:

Sub-topic	Specific claim	Author's opinion about the information		
		Completely agrees	Accepts	Leaves room for doubt
Trends in the use of TM/CAM				
Reasons for using TM/CAM in the developing world				
Reasons for using TM/CAM in the developed world				
Problems with the safety of TM/CAM				
Problems with the efficacy of TM/CAM				

b   Before the next lesson, research more material about traditional and complementary medicines which is specifically relevant to your assignment title. When you find possible sources, read them and take notes, considering what claims the authors make, and how certain they are. Then consider this in relation to other information you have gathered, to help you decide how much you accept the information they present.

Go to the checklist on p.241. Look again at the tips relating to Unit 3 Parts A–B and tick (✓) those you have used in your studies. Read the tips relating to Unit 3 Part C.

Reporting in speech

By the end of Part D you will be able to:

- explain the possible implications of events
- give an oral progress report.

1 Explaining the possible implications of events

> Events have implications – things which may be likely to happen as a result of their occurrence. Research findings often reveal new information about the world. Considering the implications that follow from this new information is useful because it allows you to develop new ideas of your own and demonstrate critical thinking.

1a Work in pairs. Read about the findings from three different research projects below. What are the possible implications of the findings in each case?

> **Project A**
>
> Researchers studying government health policies discover that government spending on medicines is declining in many developing countries.
>
> **Project B**
>
> Researchers investigating economic development discover that average per capita income is rising around the world.
>
> **Project C**
>
> Scientists working in drug development create an effective new anti-malaria drug.

1b Read the information about one student's research investigating international migration into Europe. Work in pairs. Predict the likely implications of the findings for the following.

1 Migrants wishing to move to Europe

2 Europeans

3 The culture and environment of European towns and cities

4 European government policies

> Adam is a student who has been doing a research project about migration to Europe. He has discovered that migration of non-European people into Europe has increased dramatically over the past two decades, and that the range of countries that migrants come from has widened, so that more people from different backgrounds are now living in European cities. He has also discovered that the results of a survey of developed nations' government attitudes towards immigration show that over 40% have adopted policies to reduce immigration.

1c Check your answers with another pair.

3.9

1d Listen to Adam and compare his ideas about the implications of his work with your own ideas.

> Implications are only possibilities, therefore it is important to be cautious when expressing them. Words and phrases such as 'It seems likely that' or 'It's possible that' can be used to show your level of caution when speaking about implications.

1e Look at the transcript of Adam's speech (**Appendix 6**). Identify the phrases that he uses to introduce and explain the implications, and write them in the table below.

Useful expressions for describing implications

1f Read the information about immigration to developed nations and answer these questions.

1 Overall, what is the trend in the numbers of migrants to developed nations?

2 How do residents of developed nations feel about migration?

1 In most developed nations, the share of immigrants who come from developing nations has risen dramatically. For instance, between 1960 and 1969, only about 50% of the migrants to the USA came from developing nations, while in the period 1990 to 2004, it was over 90%; similarly, only 11% of migrants to Sweden in the 1960s came from developing countries, while between 1990 and 2004, the figure was closer to 60%.

2 Though incomes are rising in many countries, overall the gap in incomes between the world's developed nations and the developing ones has widened in the past 50 years.

3 In the developing regions of the world, the percentage of the working-age population is predicted to rise sharply in the next 40 years. For instance, in Latin America, the working-age population is expected to increase by 26% by the year 2050; in Asia a 22% increase is predicted; while in Africa a 125% increase is predicted. By contrast, the working-age population in Europe is expected to fall by around 23%.

4 Unemployment is currently increasing in many developing nations.

5 One survey found that, in many nations, people tend to support immigration if they feel that there are enough jobs available (Kleemans & Klugman, 2009).

6 The same survey also found that between 50% and 60% of people in developed nations feel that ethnic diversity is beneficial for their countries.

Source: United Nations Development Programme (2009). Human Development Report 2009 - Overcoming barriers: human mobility and development. New York: UNDP.

1g Work in pairs. Use the information in the text in 1f to think about the future. Discuss the implications of this information for:

   1 Numbers of people attempting to migrate from the developing to the developed world in the future

   2 Attitudes towards immigration among residents in destination countries in the future

   3 Destination countries' future policies on migration.

1h Work in small groups. Compare your implications from 1g. Consider each suggested implication in turn and discuss which ones you think are most likely. Try to come to a group consensus about the most likely implications.

1i Present your ideas to the class. Explain which implications your group thinks are most likely, and give reasons to support your opinions.

2   Giving an oral progress report

Progress reports are given in a number of different academic and professional situations. You might, for instance, give an academic supervisor a report about how a piece of research work is progressing, or give a summary of progress about a group project to other members of that group. At work, you might give a manager a report about a project which you are conducting. In any oral progress report, you must be able to give a concise and clear summary of how the work is progressing.

2a Listen to a student giving an oral progress report. What stage of the project has been reached?

3.10

2b Listen again. Answer these questions.

   1 Who is the report being given to?

      a a workplace manager

      b a member of a project working group

      c an academic supervisor

      d a sponsor

   2 Is the project on schedule?

   3 What problems have been encountered, and what are their implications for the completion of the project?

2c Check your answers with a partner.

2d Work in pairs. Discuss what information you should include in a progress report. (You may wish to review Unit 3 Part E2 to help you.)

2e You are going to perform a role-play. Work in pairs and read the role your teacher assigns you below. Make notes on what you are going to say.

Role-play 1:

Student 1: You are a student working on a research project. You are going to give a progress report to your academic supervisor.

Project information

Research aim: you are trying to gather information about predictions of technological developments over the next 50 years. You plan to evaluate them and consider the possible implications of introducing various new technologies.

Stages of project	Estimated time required
Selecting a research question	2 weeks
Doing a literature review	3 weeks
Creating a project proposal	1 week
Gathering data	3 weeks
Collating and analyzing the data	2 weeks
Writing up first draft	3 weeks
Writing up final draft	3 weeks

Stage you had expected to reach at this point: Writing up the first draft.

Stage you have actually reached: Collating and analyzing the data. You have been doing this for around two weeks already, and you expect it will take another two weeks to complete this stage.

Key/interesting findings so far: Many sources predict increasing use of genetic engineering and growth in 'environmentally friendly' technologies.

Problems encountered: A lot of the data you found was too technical, so it's been difficult trying to understand it, and that's taken time.

When you expect to finish: You decide.

Student 2: You are an academic supervisor. You are going to listen to one of your students give a progress report on a research project that they are doing. Read the information in the box below and take a few minutes to plan what questions you are going to ask.

> ### Supervisor information
>
> Student's research aim: evaluating predictions of technological developments over the next 50 years, and considering the implications of these new technologies.
>
> Try to find out this information from your student:
>
> **1** if the project is going according to schedule
> **2** what they have discovered so far
> **3** what problems they have encountered
> **4** when the student expects to complete the work
> **5** any other questions (you decide).

Role-play 2:

Now switch roles. Student 1 listens and asks questions as Student 2 gives a progress report. Use the information on the role cards below to help you prepare for this.

Student 1: You are an academic supervisor. You are going to listen to one of your students give a progress report on a research project that they are doing. Read the information in the box below and take a few minutes to plan what questions you are going to ask.

> ### Supervisor information
>
> Student's research aim: studying the relationship between illiteracy and standard of living. The student is gathering data about illiteracy rates around the world, as well as data on salaries, employment and health, to see if standards of living are lower in nations with higher illiteracy.
>
> Try to find out this information from your student:
>
> **1** if the project is going according to schedule
> **2** what they have discovered so far
> **3** what problems they have encountered
> **4** why the problem occurred
> **5** if the student thinks they need more time to be able to complete the project
> **6** any other questions (you decide).

Student 2: You are a student working on a research project. You are going to give a progress report to your academic supervisor.

> ### Project information
>
> Research aim: you are trying to study the relationship between illiteracy and standard of living. You want to gather data about illiteracy rates around the world, as well as data on salaries, employment and health, to see if standards of living are lower in nations with higher illiteracy.

Stages of project	Time required
Selecting a research question	1 week
Doing a literature review	2 weeks
Creating a project proposal	1 week
Gathering data	3 weeks
Collating and analyzing the data	1 month
Writing up first draft	3 weeks
Writing up final draft	2 weeks

Stage you had expected to reach at this point: Collating and analyzing the data.

Stage you have actually reached: Doing a literature review.

Key findings so far: None.

Problems encountered: You've found it very difficult to find relevant literature. Many of the sources are out of date, and those which are don't seem to be clearly related to your topic.

When you expect to finish: You decide.

> **UNIT TASK** **Traditional, complementary and modern medicine**

In this unit task, you will work with a group of three or four other students to hold a discussion about different aspects of the assignment title that you have chosen. Your teacher will give you more information about how long the discussion should be.

a Read the questions under your chosen assignment title and make notes of your answers.

b Work in small groups with students who have chosen the same assignment. Discuss each of the questions in turn. Your aim in the discussion should be to contribute your own ideas, discover new information and ideas from your classmates, and investigate what their opinions are based on. Try to consider as many different aspects of the topic and alternative points of view as possible. If you feel that your own opinion differs from a classmate's, then you should use information and data from your research on the topic to attempt to persuade them that your ideas are reasonable.

Supplementary questions

Assignment title 1:

1 There is high public demand for complementary treatments. To what extent is this demand justified?

2 Are there any differences in effectiveness between different types of complementary/traditional medicines? Which ones would you be prepared to recommend?

3 What are the possible implications of using the budget for complementary medicines instead of spending it on 'modern' healthcare?

4 What are the possible implications of choosing not to spend the budget on complementary medicines?

Assignment title 2:

1 What are the main reasons for people choosing traditional/complementary medicines in the country or region you are studying?

2 There is considerable debate about whether traditional or complementary medicines are effective when compared with 'modern' Western medicine. To what extent should the use of traditional and complementary medicines be promoted?

3 What are the implications for public health when large numbers of the population rely on traditional or complementary medicines which may not have been clinically tested?

 Go to the checklist on p.241. Look again at the tips relating to Unit 3 Parts A–C and tick (✓) those you have used in your studies. Read the tips relating to Unit 3 Part D.

Reporting written Information

By the end of Part E you will be able to:
- explain, compare and interpret sources
- synthesize sources and viewpoints
- write a progress report.

1   Explaining, comparing and interpreting sources

Good academic writing is normally supported by information from other sources. This information, properly acknowledged with citations to show where it comes from, can help illustrate your ideas for your reader, as well as showing them that your opinions have been developed from careful research and are supported by other reliable sources of information.

1a   Read these statements about using sources in academic writing and tick (✓) the appropriate column of the table.

Statement	Agree	Disagree
1 When you include information from other sources, you don't need to explain what it means – the reader should be allowed to think about it for themselves.		
2 You need to be able to interpret what information from other sources means and explain how it is relevant to your own writing.		
3 You should not try to 'interpret' what information from other sources means, as you may misunderstand and give the wrong interpretation.		
4 In your writing, you should methodically present information from different sources one by one, in separate paragraphs or sections.		
5 It is the writer's responsibility to explain, compare and interpret any information from different sources to their reader.		
6 It is the reader's responsibility to understand and interpret supporting information from other sources. The writer should not explain too much.		

1b   Check your answers with a partner. Explain the reasons for your answers.

When you interpret another writer's work, you should consider these points:
- What the writer's intended meaning is
- Whether you interpret the writer's claims as supporting or contradicting your own views.

You should not deliberately misrepresent another author's claims, nor should you selectively choose only the information which supports your ideas while ignoring other data that might contradict them.

1c You are going to read about progress and development. Before you begin, work in small groups to discuss these questions.

    1 What do the words *progress* and *development* mean to you?

    2 What do you think is the best way to measure 'progress' in human life?

1d Read the text below from a source (Jones, 2008). What is Jones's idea of social progress?

Source: Jones, 2008, p.21

There are various types of 'progress' – economic, social and technological. But what is the end, the ultimate aim, of such progress? For many authors concerned with the topic of progress throughout history, the very purpose of this progress is increased human development: that progress of all sorts should enable humans to lead more satisfying lives with a decent standard of living, freedom and safety. In an intellectual current running from ancient Greece until the Enlightenment in the 18th century, we find the idea that human development is development towards greater levels of knowledge, rationality and culture. More recently, the United Nations' annual Human Development Report measures progress not in terms of industrial output or economic growth alone, but instead considers it from the point of view of the quality of life that people can enjoy; in this view, progress is determined by the percentage of people that receive education, enjoy long and healthy lives (and access to the kind of medical care that will enable them to achieve this), and have political and social freedoms. Technological and economic progress without an increase in overall human well-being cannot really be called progress at all.

1e The two texts below explain and interpret Jones's views. They were written by different students. Read each text and decide whether each student has represented Jones's views accurately or not.

Student A

According to Jones (2008, p.21), progress should be gauged not merely by technological or financial developments, but by how much the quality of people's lives is improved. Jones points out that various prominent scholars throughout history have taken the view that technological and economic progress must finally serve to support quality of life, freedom and security.

Student B

Jones (2008, p.21) states that the key to social progress – improvement in the quality of human life – is technological and economic development. Improvement in these areas is a necessary foundation for social progress of any sort, and without progress in these areas, he argues, we cannot hope to achieve developments in human society.

1f Check your answers with a partner. Give reasons for your answers.

1g Read the three sources on pp.177–178 and answer the questions about the writer's position which follow each text.

Source A: Kirkup, 2007, p.15

There is a common belief in the linearity of social progress, that 'progress' in human affairs is inevitable. This belief tends to confuse social progress – improvements in the condition of human life – with simple technological development: where there are technological developments, it is argued, there naturally follow improvements in the conditions of life. This benign view of the world, which has its foundations in the writings of Enlightenment scholars such as Voltaire and Locke, trusts in reason, rationality and the knowledge developed from scientific inquiry.

However, many authors challenge this optimistic view of progress, arguing that technical and material progress do not automatically lead to improvements in the quality of life which is experienced by many millions of people in the world. Certain events suggest precisely the opposite: technology might have advanced, but human behaviour is unchanged. This mix of technological advances with unchanged human needs and behaviours has led to severe problems and risks: the world wars of 20th century; the more modern threats of nuclear conflict and environmental degradation; these are constant reminders of the danger of putting our faith in technological progress alone. There are difficulties, too, in equating progress with economic development. Many developing countries find that high GDP growth rate has not necessarily reduced socioeconomic deprivation for large sectors of their populations. While it is undeniable that scientific, technological and economic developments have brought very real benefits to millions, if not billions, of people around the world in the course of human history, we should be cautious about equating technical and economic development with real advances in social progress.

Source A:

1   Which of these statements most accurately describes the author's position?

   a   It is false to claim that there has been social progress in the world.

   b   Economic and technological developments have rarely helped to improve the conditions of human life.

   c   We should not claim that all technological and economic progress is beneficial.

Source B: Goyal, 2010, p.237

There is a widespread view that 'progress' is inevitable: a belief in reason and scientific progress which has its roots in the Enlightenment view that scientific enquiry could lead to material and social betterment. However, as the philosopher John Gray has pointed out, the idea of social progress is a myth. The entire course of the 20th century has proven that technological development does not lead to improvements in people's lives, and often affects them for the worse: think of the devastation of the two world wars or man-made environmental catastrophes, from the US Dustbowl through the meltdown at the Chernobyl nuclear reactor, to the massive damage caused by oil spills, whether accidental, as in the case of the recent oil leak in the Gulf of Mexico, or intentional, such as the deliberate firing of oil wells in the aftermath of the Persian Gulf War.

Another dearly held view of those who believe in the idea of constant progress is that economic development will automatically lead to social improvement, but disastrous falls in the stock market, such as the Wall Street Crash of 1929, or the more recent stock market troubles of 2008, demonstrated that the trend of financial development is not always up. Furthermore, the continued and intractable existence of poverty should give us pause before we make claims about the powers of the economy to improve people's lives. By the start of the 21st century, the gap between the world's rich and poor had massively increased, with the have-nots condemned to even worse conditions in the future.

Source B:

1 Which of these statements most accurately describes the author's position? More than one answer may be possible.

   a It is false to claim that there has been social progress in the world.

   b Economic and technological developments have rarely helped to improve the conditions of human life.

   c We should not claim that all technological and economic progress is beneficial.

Source C: Maxwell, 2010, p.18

It has become fashionable of late to question whether 'progress' exists. A number of commentators of the more pessimistic sort insist that technological development, far from helping to improve our lives, only tends to cause more social problems than it relieves. This tendency, they claim, is made worse by prevailing economic conditions which favour the wealthy at the expense of the poor, and create a social climate in which economic gain is pursued without consideration for any negative consequences. However, while there is clearly an element of truth in these claims, the simple fact is that progress – a constant improvement in the human condition – is an observable fact in the world around us. Developments in science and technology, for instance, have given us advanced medical treatment, or the ability to communicate and share our thoughts and ideas with like-minded people on the other side of the world. Our creative capacities have been massively enhanced by the development first of printed literature and later computers and the Internet. Though poverty still clearly exists, the trend is towards an improvement of GDP throughout the world, affording more people the possibility, or at least the hope, of improvements in their quality of life. Where technological and economic progress goes, so too does social progress. Improvements in medicine or information technology, for instance, are not merely technical developments: they also create very real improvements in human social conditions, and where people are healthier, richer and empowered by education, they in turn can contribute to greater progress for the generations that follow them.

That this progress exists is beyond doubt, though undeniably the course is often slow, and there have been occasions where it seems to have been reversed. We cannot overlook the fact that our technology is implicated in certain tragic episodes in our history: the devastation of most modern wars is only possible with the industrial production of weaponry, for instance. We are also reminded of the place of technology in environmental disasters such as the fatal Bhopal disaster in India in 1984, or the meltdown of the Chernobyl nuclear reactor in 1986, or still more recently the BP oil spill in the Gulf of Mexico. These were all, clearly, events where the negative consequences of our technologies became clear. Nevertheless, we should not look at isolated disasters and say that they are the sum of human experience. The trend is ever upwards.

Source C:

1 Which of these statements most accurately describes the author's position?

   a Social, technological and economic progress are all linked, and help in human development.

   b Economic and technological developments have rarely helped to improve the conditions of human life.

   c Technological and economic development always result in social progress.

1h Work in pairs. Discuss your interpretation of the author's position. Discuss to what extent you agree with each of the author's claims.

1i Read the text on p.179 written by a student, interpreting Source A, and make notes on how it might be improved.

> *The evidence of progress in human affairs is everywhere: around the world, billions enjoy higher standards of living, access to nourishing food and clean water, better educational and employment prospects, and protections of their freedoms and rights. These improvements in the human condition are safeguarded by organizations such as the United Nations, and it is arguably true that the ideal of human development is shared by all. However, some sceptics claim that this is not in fact the case. Kirkup (2007), for instance, claims that economic and technological developments have not led to greater positive progress in human affairs, and have in fact often had the reverse effect. He claims that the main results of technological development have been the catastrophic wars of the 20th century and damage to the environment.*

1j Write an improved version of the explanation which more accurately represents the writer's position in Source A.

1k Comparisons of different authors' positions are common in academic writing. The text below has been written by a student to compare Sources B and C on pp.177–178. Read it and decide whether the student has interpreted each source's intended meaning accurately and fairly. Make notes about how they could improve any misrepresentations of the sources' positions.

> There is a widespread view that the direction of history is a straight, upwards progression of ever-improving technological and social conditions. However, there is in fact some debate about the extent to which social progress really takes place. Goyal, for instance, claims that social progress is a 'myth' (Goyal, 2010, p.237). He asserts that undoubted developments in technology and the growth of financial markets have not helped to relieve poverty or suffering, and have instead led to catastrophic wars and environmental breakdown.
>
> A similar view is held by Maxwell (2010), who notes that a number of prominent commentators now question the idea that real social progress exists at all when it is coupled with extensive environmental and social breakdown. Maxwell also notes that there have been frequent 'reversals' of progress in history, including the First and Second World Wars in the 20th century, environmental disasters such as Bhopal, Chernobyl and the BP oil spill in the Gulf of Mexico.

1l Write an improved version of the second paragraph which more accurately explains and compares each of the two sources.

> Maxwell (2010) takes a different view.

1m Work in pairs. Compare your writing. To what extent do you agree with your partner's interpretation and comparison of the two sources?

2 Synthesizing sources and viewpoints

> Your written work should be an expression of your own understanding of a topic. However, in order to be academically acceptable this must be based on your understanding and interpretation of the sources you read. Your writing therefore should be a synthesis of your own views and supporting information from other sources. You should be able to demonstrate how your understanding relates to the expert sources that you have used for information. Both your own ideas and the information from other sources should be expressed in your own words as much as possible.

2a Work in small groups. Discuss these questions.

1 Do you agree that the quality of human life is always improving? Why?

2 What are some of the biggest advantages of technology?

3 What are some of the biggest disadvantages of technology?

2b Read this excerpt from a student's essay and make a note of the main idea of each paragraph in the table.

Excerpt	Main idea of paragraph
1 The idea of progress in history is often taken for granted (Wirth, 2009). However, there are issues with this view of constant upward progress which raise questions about whether scientific and technological progress equates to true improvements in the human condition.	
2 Beginning in the 19th century, awareness of the negative consequences of industrialization became more widespread, and the notion of technological advance as being a uniform good came to be questioned. In Britain, the shift to an industrial economy brought rapid demographic changes as the workforce moved into ever-larger cities to work in manufacturing industries. This trend towards urbanization brought with it other ills – crowded living conditions, poor hygiene and standards of living overall (Wirth, 2009, p.106). Urbanization has been a feature of human life in all societies, both developing and developed, ever since.	

3

The experiences of the 20th century have added to the unease with which technological development is viewed. The great advances in science, technology and social organization which were expected to have led to a better future for mankind instead resulted in two of the most destructive wars ever known and ushered in the nuclear age which, despite its promise of limitless energy, of course also brought with it the threat of nuclear conflict (Wirth, 2009, p.342). In the course of the 20th century, humankind has also become more aware of the negative environmental consequences of technological progress; a number of significant environmental disasters brought home to people the fact that technological progress often came at a high price. One famous example was the enormous damage caused to Alaskan wildlife in 1989 when the oil tanker Exxon Valdez ran aground in a sheltered harbour, spilling an estimated 600,000 barrels of oil and causing grave damage both to the ecosystem and the local economy (Wirth, 2009, p.267). Interestingly, the Exxon Valdez spill was fairly modest compared to many other 20th-century oil spills (Wirth, 2009, p.268), but it helped raise awareness of the environmental consequences of technological development because another technology – television – helped to spread the news of the spill, and graphic images of its effects, around the world.

4

As events have shown, the course of human development has not been one of uniform positive progress. Wirth (2009, p.18) points out that the development of increasingly powerful technologies without change in human behaviour or patterns of consumption will inevitably prevent true progress, because quality of life will increasingly be diminished for the majority of people through war, environmental degradation and want. Nevertheless, it is undeniable that technological and economic growth has enabled a very real social progress and improvements in the quality of life for vast numbers of people. Very real improvements in the human condition have taken place since the Industrial Revolution. These include material advances such as rising incomes and access to labour-saving technologies, as well as improvements in health – such as increased life expectancy – in many countries (Wirth, 2009, p.96).

3c Use the information below to create a progress report email to your supervisor.

Today's date:

17 June

Overview of aim

To evaluate consumers' opinions about over-the-counter herbal medicines.

Original completion schedule

Selection of research question – by 1 June

Completion of initial literature review – 19 June

Submission of project proposal – 28 June

Completion of data collection – 14 July

Analysis of data – 28 July

First draft – 15 August

Revision and final draft – 6 September

How much complete so far

Literature review only partially completed.

Have started recruiting respondents.

Have drafted the questionnaire for use with the respondents.

Problems encountered

Difficult to find information relating to the topic. The relevant material is not in the university library, and you are still waiting to get an interlibrary loan. Also, the journal articles you found were not as relevant as you had expected.

What is currently being done

Looking for more relevant sources and waiting for a loan. Planning a trip to a different university library to borrow the books which they have.

What remains to be done

Finish reading and note-taking by 24 June.

Draft initial literature review by 29 June.

Submit project proposal by 3 July.

All other tasks as listed in the original schedule.

To:	Dr P Hopkins<p.hopkins@tctu.ac.uk.>
From:	
Subject:	Progress on research project

Dear Dr Hopkins,

Best wishes,

3d Compare your report with a partner. Identify the sections in your partner's report.

➤ **UNIT TASK** **Traditional, complementary and modern medicine**

a Having completed your research and participated in a discussion about different approaches to medicine, in this unit task you will write a short report on the assignment title of your choice. (Your teacher will tell you how long this report should be.)

b Plan your report. Make notes in the table below.

Key background information for introduction:	
Main body sections:	
Main idea	**Supporting information**
1	
2	
3	
4	

Your report should be based on an appropriate synthesis of your own ideas and supporting information from expert sources. Use quotation, paraphrasing and summary to incorporate other writers' work into your report. You should give proper citations and references (following the Harvard format that you have learned in this book) for any ideas or information you use from other sources.

 Go to the checklist on p.241. Look again at the tips relating to Unit 3 Parts A–D and tick (✓) those you have used in your studies. Read the tips relating to Unit 3 Part E.

Unit 4 Art, creativity and design

Unit overview

Part	This part will help you to ...	By improving your ability to ...
A	**Listen actively**	• cope with distractions • detect a speaker's level of certainty • listen critically.
B	**Read intensively**	• identify appropriate reading techniques • read intensively for understanding • read critically.
C	**Evaluate the strength of research evidence**	• understand reliability and validity • analyze the suitability of samples.
D	**Discuss research findings**	• describe research findings • describe and explain data • discuss research findings.
E	**Write a formal report**	• use supporting information in writing • write an abstract • avoid plagiarism.

Understanding spoken information

By the end of Part A you will be able to:

- cope with distractions
- detect a speaker's level of certainty
- listen critically.

1 Coping with distractions

> Listening effectively in an academic context is often made more difficult by distractions – things going on around you, or even off-topic thoughts, which make it more difficult for you to focus on what a speaker is saying.

1a Read the list of possible distractions in the table below and, for each one, decide how serious you consider each distraction to be for you on a scale of 1–5 (1 = a minor distraction, 5 = a very serious distraction).

Distractions	Seriousness				
	1	2	3	4	5
Strange behaviour by the speaker (e.g. pacing or fidgeting)					
Something unusual or striking about the speaker's appearance or dress					
Other people talking at the same time as the speaker					
Other audience members clearly not paying attention to the speaker (e.g. listening to music, checking a mobile phone, passing notes to each other)					
Other things going on in your life					
Lack of interest in the topic					
The temperature of the room					
The speaker's accent					
Your own physical comfort					
Whether the speaker stays on topic or talks about something off topic					

1b Is there anything else which you find distracting? If so, add your ideas to the list in 1a.

1c Work in small groups and share your ideas. Discuss whether you find the same things distracting. Can you think of any methods for avoiding or ignoring the distractions?

2 Detecting a speaker's level of certainty

> Listening actively does not mean simply being able to understand the speaker's intended meaning. As an active listener, you should also be able to identify and evaluate the speaker's position on a topic, and your own judgment about it.

2a The expressions below can indicate how certain a speaker is about the claims they make. Decide which expressions show greater certainty about a claim (C) and which leave room for doubt (D).

Expressions	C or D
1 This proves that ...	
2 ... definitely ...	
3 This suggests that ...	
4 Perhaps ...	
5 It is clear that ...	
6 It tends to ...	
7 The evidence indicates that ...	
8 It is not true.	
9 ... obviously ...	
10 It may not always be the case.	
11 It seems to ...	
12 In fact ...	

2b Check your answers with a partner.

2c Marketers and advertisers use research about ideas of human beauty when they try to appeal to customers. Advertisers can choose to use 'highly attractive models' (HAMs) or 'normally attractive models' (NAMs) to sell their products. Work in pairs. Discuss which type of model would be most effective for selling these products. Give reasons for your ideas.
- Soap and toothpaste
- Cars
- Jewellery
- Chocolate
- Airline travel

4.1

2d Listen to two speakers make claims about how marketers and advertizers use
models when trying to appeal to customers. Complete these notes.

Speaker 1	**1 Effectiveness of HAMs overall?**
	2 Bower and Landreth 2001: a) HAMS = good for: b) NAMS = good for:
Speaker 2	**1 Effectiveness of HAMs overall?** **2 Bower and Landreth 2001** a) Consumers trust HAMS? b) Adverts are most effective if consumer can believe that ... **3 Kamins 1990** a) Best models for clothes, jewellery, etc. = b) Best for food, furniture polish, etc. = **4 Effect of attractiveness overall?**

2e From the list below, choose one statement for each speaker that best summarizes their position on the topic.

    1 The speaker believes that it does not matter whether an advertising model is beautiful or not.

    2 The speaker believes that NAMs *may* be more useful for selling ordinary products than HAMs.

    3 The speaker believes that NAMs *are definitely* more useful for selling ordinary products than HAMs.

    4 The speaker believes that people *may* distrust HAMs.

2f Check your answers with a partner. Give reasons for your choice.

4.2

2g You are going to listen to another speaker give a talk on the subject of beauty in advertising. Listen and complete the table by making a note of how certain the speaker seems to be about each claim.

Claim	Speaker's level of certainty
People respond positively to adverts using highly attractive models.	
People from different cultural backgrounds share ideas about what is 'beautiful'.	

4.2

2h Listen to the talk again. While you listen, look at these statements. Which statement best summarizes the speaker's stance on the topic as a whole?

    1 The speaker strongly believes that people are more influenced by beautiful models used for advertising.

    2 The speaker believes that the apparent beauty of a model may have some influence on consumers.

    3 The speaker believes that people are not very greatly affected by the apparent beauty of a model used for advertising.

2i Check your answers with a partner. Give reasons for the answer you chose.

3 Listening critically

> Understanding the speaker's certainty about their own claims is only one part of listening critically. You should also be able to judge for yourself whether you accept the claims that the speaker is making. Some speakers may not show any uncertainty in the expressions that they use; this does not mean that you should accept the information without question.

4.2

3a Listen again to the lecture from Part 2g. Work in pairs to answer these questions to help you decide if the speaker's claims are justified.

    1 To what extent does the evidence given support the claim that the speaker makes?

2 Are the statistics which are used from trustworthy sources?

3 Does the evidence given support the speaker's conclusions?

4 Can you think of any alternative conclusions which the speaker has not mentioned?

4.3

3b Listen to another speaker make claims on a similar topic and write notes in the table.

Theme of talk:		
Claims:		**Supporting points:**
1 Notions of what a 'beautiful' person is clearly vary between different cultures.		
2 Criteria for judging beauty vary from place to place vary.		USA: Taiwan and Singapore:
3 Advertising within a culture is simpler than advertising between cultures.		

3c Compare your notes with a partner.

4.3

3d Listen again. Pay attention to the way that the speaker expresses their claims. How certain is the speaker about the strength of the claims that they make?

3e Consider your own response to the claims. Use the questions in activity 3a above to help you decide whether the speaker's certainty is justified.

3f Discuss your ideas with a partner.

Designing buildings for human needs

The Unit 4 task is about the factors involved in the design of modern living and work spaces. At the end of each part, you will be asked to complete a stage of the task as follows:

Part A: Listen to an introduction on the topic.

Part B: Read a text about it.

Part C: Do some further research for relevant material.

Part D: Have a group discussion on the topic.

Part E: Write a report with one of these titles:

Assignment 1

Write a report outlining the factors which should be taken into account in the design of a modern living or work space. Illustrate your claims with evidence from research on the topic. Make recommendations about how a possible 'ideal' space for a specific purpose (e.g. relaxing, working, cooking) might be designed.

Assignment 2

A university is planning to design a new accommodation hall for students. The university has specified that each room should offer both a comfortable and relaxing living environment, as well as conditions that are suitable for study. Bearing this in mind, write a report identifying the elements that should be taken into account, and making recommendations about how the rooms should be arranged.

a You are going to listen to a short general introduction to some of the considerations involved in the design of modern living and work spaces. Before you listen, work in groups. Discuss these questions.

    1 What factors might be considered in the design of a modern work space?

    2 What factors might be considered in the design of a modern living space?

    3 What elements of a room's design might contribute to a positive mood in its occupants?

b Work in small groups with other students who have chosen the same assignment title as you. Briefly discuss your ideas about the assignment title.

c Listen and write notes of the speaker's main points and claims in the table.

4.4

Main idea of the talk:	
Sub-topic:	**Claim:**
Environmental considerations	
Affective factors	
Practical factors	

d Listen again. Pay attention to the way the speaker makes the claims. How certain is the speaker?

e Work in pairs. Spend some time reflecting on your notes. Discuss to what extent you accept the claims made by the speaker.

f Work in small groups again to share the information that you heard. How does the information you heard relate to the assignment title you have chosen?

 Go to the checklist on p.241 and read the tips relating to Unit 4 Part A.

Unit 4
Part B

Understanding written information

By the end of Part B you will be able to:
- identify appropriate reading techniques
- read intensively for understanding
- read critically.

1 Identifying appropriate reading techniques

1a Work in small groups. Cover the text below. Discuss these questions.

    1 What types of reading technique have you learned about before?

    2 What does 'intensive reading' mean to you?

1b Read the definition of *intensive reading* to check whether your ideas in 1a are correct.

> Intensive reading is one reading technique which is vital in academic study. Intensive reading is what you do when you read something – a sentence, paragraph or even a whole text – very carefully to be sure that you have understood all the details and understand exactly what the author means. Because the aim of intensive reading is complete and accurate understanding, it is normal to read slowly and ask yourself whether your understanding is correct; you may need to re-read several times or check words you don't understand in a dictionary.

1c Work in pairs. Discuss the differences between intensive reading and the techniques of *skimming* and *scanning*.

1d Tick (✓) the reading styles that seem most appropriate for each situation (more than one answer is possible).

Situation	Reading style		
	Skimming	Scanning	Intensive
1 You are looking in the index of a book to see if it contains any information about Renaissance art.			
2 You have read a relevant article, and though you understand the gist of the article, there is a paragraph on p.2 which you can't understand.			
3 You are trying to understand the instructions for a lab experiment.			
4 You have to read some safety instructions before beginning a lab session.			

5 You have read through two sources on the same topic. They seem to have the same ideas, but your teacher told you that in fact there are important differences between them.

6 You are writing an essay about Renaissance art. You have a book titled *An Introduction to Art: Theory and History* and you want to find out if there is any useful background information on the topic which you could include in your essay.

7 You are going to take part in a seminar about *contrapposto* in classical art. You need to find out exactly what this means so that you can contribute to the seminar.

2 Reading intensively for understanding

2a Work in small groups. Discuss these questions about art.

    1 How many different types of visual art (e.g. a sketch) can you think of?

    2 Do you like looking at works of art? What styles of art do you like (e.g. Medieval, Renaissance, Modern)?

    3 Is there any type of art you dislike? Why?

2b Work in pairs. Match the three examples of European art from different ages with the correct place on the timeline below. Discuss which, if any, of the three artworks you prefer. Explain your reasons.

Classical period Approx. 8th century BC – 5th century AD   Middle Ages Approx. 5th–14th centuries AD   Renaissance Approx. 15th–17th centuries AD

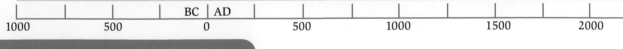

2c You are going to practise reading intensively by comparing two versions of the same text closely. There are slight differences between them. Read the first text and complete the notes about the author's main idea and any supporting information they give.

A

Nowhere in Europe created more *beautiful*, or *realistic*, art than Italy in the fifteenth and sixteenth centuries. This period is known as the Renaissance, or 'revival', because it abandoned the unaccomplished, or near-primitive, art of the Middle Ages (the period between the Classical Age of ancient Greece and Rome, and the Renaissance) and revived the magnificent art of classical Italy. Classical art was more 'real' than art in the Middle Ages because it captured a genuine image of the human form: people looked like real people. Italian Renaissance artists revived this reality, or 'truth', in their art, but were only able to do so through reference to classical writing on proportion and contemporary Italian scientific discoveries about perspective. Mathematics taught Italian artists how to recreate nature's beauty in sculpture, architecture and paintings: human beings were represented with accurate proportions; landscapes were recreated on flat walls as though a window had been opened to the world. Meanwhile, art in Northern Europe was unaffected by Renaissance teachings. Art continued to be created in a flat, less true-to-life manner. Jan van Eyck (1390?–1441), of the Netherlands, did try to make his paintings realistic, copying minute detail such as individual hairs in an animal's fur and strands in a tapestry to make his images seem true-to-life, but did not accurately recreate the world using the Italian techniques of perspective or proportion. Though Jan van Eyck attempted to make his painting beautiful and realistic through making his art colourful and detailed, his art was less effective in terms of beauty and reality than his Italian counterparts'.

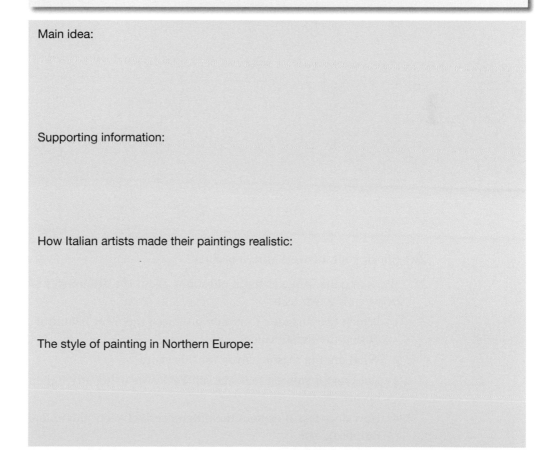

Main idea:

Supporting information:

How Italian artists made their paintings realistic:

The style of painting in Northern Europe:

2d Read a slightly altered version of text A. What differences can you spot between the two texts? Read and write notes.

B

Europe created *beautiful*, and *realistic*, art in the fifteenth and sixteenth centuries. This period is known as the Renaissance, or 'revival', because it moved away from the less lifelike art of the Middle Ages (the period between the Classical Age of ancient Greece and Rome, and the Renaissance) and revived the more true-to-life art of classical times. Classical art was thought to be more 'real' than art in the Middle Ages because it aimed to capture a genuine image of the human form: people looked like real people. Renaissance artists revived this reality, or 'truth', in their art, with classical writing on proportion and contemporary Italian scientific discoveries about perspective, helping to make this possible. Mathematics assisted artists in the recreation of nature's beauty in sculpture, architecture and paintings: human beings could be represented with accurate proportions; landscapes could be recreated on flat walls as though a window had been opened to the world. Meanwhile, art in Northern Europe was less affected by Renaissance teachings. While some art continued to be created in a flat, less true-to-life manner, Jan van Eyck (1390?–1441), of the Netherlands, did try to make his paintings realistic. He copied minute detail such as individual hairs in an animal's fur and strands in a tapestry to make his images seem true-to-life, but did not try to recreate the world only by using the Italian techniques of perspective or proportion. Jan van Eyck did make his painting beautiful and realistic through making his art colourful and detailed, with his art no less effective in terms of beauty and reality than his Italian counterparts'.

Source: Henstock, 2010.

Differences between the texts

2e Check your answers with a partner.

2f Work in pairs. Answer these questions about the differences in the meaning between the two texts.

1 Which text suggests that Italy produced the most beautiful and realistic art during the Renaissance?

2 What are the reasons given for this claim?

3 Does text B suggest that Jan van Eyck was using any Italian techniques in his art?

4 How does text B explain the differences between Italian and Northern European art?

5 Which text gives a more balanced view? How?